Regional Responses to U.S.-China Competition in the Indo-Pacific

Singapore

Cortez A. Cooper III and Michael S. Chase

Prepared for the United States Air Force
Approved for public release; distribution unlimited

RAND PROJECT AIR FORCE

For more information on this publication, visit www.rand.org/t/RR4412z5

For more information on this series, visit www.rand.org/US-PRC-influence

Library of Congress Cataloging-in-Publication Data is available for this publication.

ISBN: 978-1-9774-0559-3

Published by the RAND Corporation, Santa Monica, Calif.

Cover: globe: jcrosemann/GettyImages; flags: luzitanija/Adobe Stock

Preface

This report on Singapore is part of a project examining the perspectives of U.S. allies and partners in the Indo-Pacific as they formulate and implement their responses to China's more assertive foreign and security policy and to a more competitive U.S.-China relationship. Singapore views its partnership with the United States as essential to its security policy. It sees the U.S. regional presence as playing an indispensable role in ensuring its ability to navigate a regional security environment that is increasingly complicated by China's growing influence and more-assertive Chinese behavior. At the same time, China is Singapore's most important trading partner, and Singapore aims to maintain a stable relationship with China even as it pushes back against Chinese influence and interference. Singapore's deepening engagement in the region creates opportunities for the United States and, specifically, for the U.S. Department of Defense and U.S. Air Force to work with Singapore and with regional partners in new and innovative ways. The other reports in this series are available at www.rand.org/US-PRC-influence.

The research reported here was sponsored by Brig Gen Michael P. Winkler (PACAF/A5/8) and conducted within the Strategy and Doctrine Program of RAND Project AIR FORCE as part of a fiscal year 2019 project titled "Regional Responses to U.S.-China Competition in the Indo-Pacific" that assists the Air Force in evaluating U.S. and Chinese influence and assessing possible Air Force, joint force, and U.S. government options. Research was completed in October 2019.

RAND Project AIR FORCE

RAND Project AIR FORCE (PAF), a division of the RAND Corporation, is the Department of the Air Force's (DAF's) federally funded research and development center for studies and analyses. PAF provides the DAF with independent analyses of policy alternatives affecting the development, employment, combat readiness, and support of current and future air, space, and cyber forces. Research is conducted in four programs: Strategy and Doctrine, Force Modernization and Employment; Manpower, Personnel, and Training; and Resource Management. The research reported here was prepared under contract FA7014-16-D-1000.

Additional information about PAF is available on our website:
www.rand.org/paf/

This report documents work originally shared with the Department of the Air Force on September 26, 2019. The draft report, issued on March 11, 2020, was reviewed by formal peer reviewers and DAF subject-matter experts.

Contents

Figures

Tables

Summary

Issue

This report is part of a broader project that assesses the perspectives of U.S. allies and partners in the Indo-Pacific as they formulate and implement their responses to China's more assertive foreign and security policy behavior in the region and to a more competitive U.S.-China relationship. The project also examines how the U.S. Department of Defense (DoD), particularly the U.S. Air Force (USAF), can best deepen and improve its ability to work with allies and partners to maintain U.S. advantage in long-term strategic competition with China.

In this report, we assess the impact of the changes in China's strategic behavior and U.S.-China relations over the past decade on Singapore in terms of its security policies and relationships in the Indo-Pacific region. We focus on two key analytical questions:

1. How does Singapore view China's more assertive behavior and increased U.S.-China competition, and how is its government responding?
2. How should the United States work with Singapore to counter Chinese influence and protect common interests in the Indo-Pacific region?

Approach

We draw from a variety of primary and secondary sources, data sets, and (most importantly) interviews with U.S., allied, and partner government and military officials, as well as academic experts. To understand regional responses to competition, we traveled to Singapore and interviewed experts there.

Conclusions

We present the following key findings from our analysis:

- Singapore views its relations and partnership with the United States as essential to its security policy. It sees the U.S. regional presence as playing an indispensable role in ensuring its ability to navigate a regional security environment that is increasingly complicated by China's growing influence and more-assertive Chinese behavior.
- At the same time, China is Singapore's most important trading partner, and Singapore aims to maintain a stable relationship with China even as it pushes back against Chinese influence and interference.
- Singapore has deep regional engagement focused on its role as a small but influential economic and political player in the Association of Southeast Asian Nations (ASEAN). Although Singapore promotes "ASEAN centrality" in regional economic, diplomatic, and security policy issues, it also has expanded engagement on multiple fronts with actors outside ASEAN's membership.

- Over the past decade, there have been significant changes to the regional security architecture of the Indo-Pacific. An evolving web of relationships is taking shape, moving the region beyond the traditional "hub-and-spoke" system of bilateral security alliances with the United States.
- Singapore is involved as a key security partner for the United States but also as an independent actor seeking a wide variety of security ties and relationships. It has significant partnerships with Australia and India and increasing security ties with China and Japan.
- Singapore has been and remains a strategic partner for U.S. diplomacy and security efforts in Southeast Asia and the Indo-Pacific region more broadly. To sustain this success in ways that will buttress U.S. competitive advantage will require a steady hand at the helm of the relationship, strengthening ties across economic and security domains while recognizing the importance to Singapore of stable relations with and growing economic ties to China.
- Singapore's geographic location astride the Straits of Malacca, its outsize influence in ASEAN, and the military support afforded to the United States by infrastructure and access in Singapore make investments in U.S. attention and treasure both necessary and worthwhile.
- Singapore's engagement in the region creates opportunities and challenges for the United States. Opportunities continue to outweigh the challenges, specifically for DoD and the USAF to work with Singapore and with regional partners in new and innovative ways, both operationally and using soft-power tools and approaches.

Recommendations

For Pacific Air Forces and the USAF:

- Incrementally increase the current trajectory of both security assistance and operational interface (training, exercises, arms sales).
- Work with Singapore on humanitarian assistance and disaster relief and other traditional and nontraditional security activities.

For the Joint Force:

- Further enhance U.S.-Singapore cooperation in the areas of space, advanced cyber, electronic warfare, and command, control, communications, computers, intelligence, surveillance, and reconnaissance.
- Strengthen U.S.-Singapore cooperation on research and development of advanced capabilities, such as artificial intelligence.

For the U.S. government at large:

- Continue to encourage Singapore's growing cooperation and engagement with other U.S. allies, such as Australia and Japan, and emerging partners, such as India and Indonesia.
- Deliberately seek opportunities to work with Singapore to counter Chinese political interference and influence operations.
- Work with Singapore to publicly highlight China's problematic behavior in the South China Sea and elsewhere.

Acknowledgments

The authors wish to thank Brig Gen Michael P. Winkler and the entire team at Pacific Air Force (A5/8) for sponsoring this research. The authors also thank the numerous officials, analysts, and scholars in the United States and Singapore who generously shared their time and insights throughout the project. The authors are also grateful to Paula Thornhill, Raphael Cohen, Bonny Lin, Matthew Lane, Prashanth Parameswaran, and Karl Mueller for their helpful reviews of draft versions of the report.

Abbreviations

AIIB	Asia Infrastructure Investment Bank
ASEAN	Association of Southeast Asian Nations
BRI	Belt and Road Initiative
CPTPP	Comprehensive and Progressive Agreement for Trans-Pacific Partnership
DoD	U.S. Department of Defense
FDI	foreign direct investment
FOIP	Free and Open Indo-Pacific
HA/DR	humanitarian assistance and disaster relief
ISIS	Islamic State in Iraq and Syria
JSPP21	Japan-Singapore Partnership Programme for the 21st Century
PRC	People's Republic of China
RCEP	Regional Comprehensive Economic Partnership
RSAF	Republic of Singapore Air Force
SCS	South China Sea
TPP	Trans-Pacific Partnership
UN	United Nations
USAF	United States Air Force

1. Singapore in the Context of U.S.-China Competition

The U.S. Department of Defense's (DoD's) *2018 National Defense Strategy* highlights the important role that U.S. allies and partners play in U.S.-China strategic competition. America's strong and enduring relationships with its allies and partners offer the United States distinct advantages in long-term competition with China: The United States is not competing with China on its own, but can draw from allied and partner resources, capabilities, and strengths that far exceed what China can bring to bear. As DoD focuses on long-term strategic competition with China, it must understand how U.S. allies and partners are responding and adjusting their approaches in the Indo-Pacific region. This is especially important because how effectively the United States works with allies and partners will be critical to determining whether the United States will be successful in maintaining its strategic advantage in the competition with China.

This report on Singapore is part of a project that examines the perspectives of U.S. allies and partners in the Indo-Pacific as they formulate and implement their responses to China's more assertive foreign and security policy behavior in the region and to a more competitive U.S.-China relationship. We also assess how DoD (particularly, the U.S. Air Force [USAF]) can best deepen and improve its ability to work with allies and partners to maintain U.S. advantage in long-term strategic competition with China.

Drawing on a review of government documents, academic articles, media reports, public opinion polls, and interviews with more than 20 officials and experts in the United States and Singapore, we explore these issues with particular attention to how Singapore is responding to growing strategic competition between the United States and China and how Washington can work together more effectively with Singapore in pursuit of shared diplomatic, economic, and security interests.

Applying the Project Framework to Singapore

The research team involved with this yearlong project developed a framework that is applied to each of the country case studies, highlighting major diplomatic and political, economic, and military and security factors relevant to understanding the responses of key countries to China's growing power and influence and U.S.-China competition over the past decade. We define U.S.-China competition for influence as focused on shaping partner choices to support U.S. objectives. We conceptualize *influence* as dependent on (1) the extent of *shared interests*—defined to include objectives, values, beliefs, and ideology—between the partner and the United States or China and (2) the capability of the United States or China to incentivize and coerce the partner. Because partners can choose to support the United States, China, or both, we focus on relative U.S. influence compared with Chinese influence (instead of U.S. influence in isolation or in absolute terms).

Table 1.1 lists 14 variables we considered in assessing relative U.S. and Chinese influence. It includes eight indicators of shared interests and six measures of relative capabilities.

Table 1.1. Variables for Assessing Relative U.S.-China Influence

Source of Influence	Type	Description
Diplomatic and political		
Diplomatic and political ties	Shared interest	How diplomatically and politically important the United States or China is to the partner and the extent of diplomatic ties
Support for U.S. versus Chinese vision for the region	Shared interest	How the partner's views of the ideal regional order aligns with the U.S. vision for the region and U.S. values versus assessed Chinese vision and values for the region
Views of U.S. commitment to the region	Shared interest	How confident (or not confident) the partner is about U.S. commitment or staying power in the region
Public opinion	Shared interest	Relative public perceptions of favorability of the United States versus China
Economic		
Economic dependence	Relative capability	The partner's current economic dependence on the United States versus China, measured by aggregating trade, investment, and tourism
Economic opportunity	Relative capability	How much the partner believes the United States versus China can provide future economic benefits
Threat perceptions of the United States versus China (economic)	Relative capability	How much the partner views U.S. or Chinese economic influence as potentially threatening, subversive, or coercive
Willingness to work with the United States versus China based on economic threat perceptions	Shared interest	Whether the partner's economic threat perception encourages it to work more with the United States or China to balance against the other economically
Military and security		
Threat perceptions of the United States versus China (military)	Relative capability	How much the partner views the United States or China as a military or security threat
Willingness to work with the United States versus China based on military threat perceptions	Shared interest	Whether the partner's military threat perception encourages it to work more with the United States or China to balance against the other militarily
Support for major U.S.-led security efforts	Shared interest	How much the partner generally supports the United States on security issues through its participation in or opposition to major U.S.-led international or regional security efforts
Military cooperation	Relative capability	How much the partner is working closely with the United States versus China militarily
U.S. versus Chinese military capability	Relative capability	How the partner views U.S. versus Chinese military capability
Perception of U.S. willingness to aid partner in conflict with China	Shared interest	How confident (or not confident) the partner is about U.S. willingness to come to its military defense in a potential conflict involving China

NOTE: Variables measuring shared interests are roman, and variables measuring relative capability are italicized.

Like the other reports that are part of this broader project, this report examines the evolution of this set of variables over a period of roughly a decade and projects how developments in these areas might unfold over the next five to ten years. The project focused on examining these variables across these periods to explore the impact of growing Chinese power and influence and the intensification of U.S.-China competition on the views and policies of U.S. allies and partners as they adjust their approaches to the United States, China, and the region. Figure 1.1 provides our findings and displays these assessments with respect to Singapore in 2019. The assessments depicted use the information and analysis in the following sections. Given the mix of qualitative and quantitative variables, the study uses five categories and corresponding colors to capture the broad differences in influence:

- *Significantly more U.S. influence* (blue): The United States has significantly more influence than China. For the quantitative variables, this is coded as a greater than 20 percent U.S. advantage in influence compared with China.
- *More U.S. influence* (light blue): The United States has moderately more influence than China. For the quantitative variables, this is coded as a 3 percent to 20 percent U.S. advantage.
- *Similar U.S. and Chinese influence* (gray): The United States has similar levels of influence as China. For the quantitative variables, this is coded as the United States having influence within 3 percent of Chinese influence.
- *More Chinese influence* (light red): China has moderately more influence than the United States. For the quantitative variables, this is coded as a 3 percent to 20 percent Chinese advantage.
- *Significantly more Chinese influence* (red): China has significantly more influence than the United States. For the quantitative variables, this is coded as a greater than 20 percent Chinese advantage.[1]

The study uses qualitative assessments for ten of the variables and quantitative data for four of the variables. The most difficult to measure are the qualitative variables:

- diplomatic and political ties
- support for U.S. versus Chinese vision for the region
- views of U.S. commitment to the region
- threat perceptions of U.S. versus China (economic or military)
- willingness to work with the United States or China based on threat perceptions (economic or military)
- economic opportunity
- perception of U.S. willingness to aid Singapore in a conflict versus China
- U.S. versus People's Republic of China (PRC) military capability.

For these variables, we account for views of the top leaders, views of the government bureaucracy, and views of the public.

---

[1] The appendix provides a detailed description of the framework coding approach and the sources (qualitative and quantitative) for the coding.

Figure 1.1. Relative U.S. and Chinese Influence in Singapore (2019)

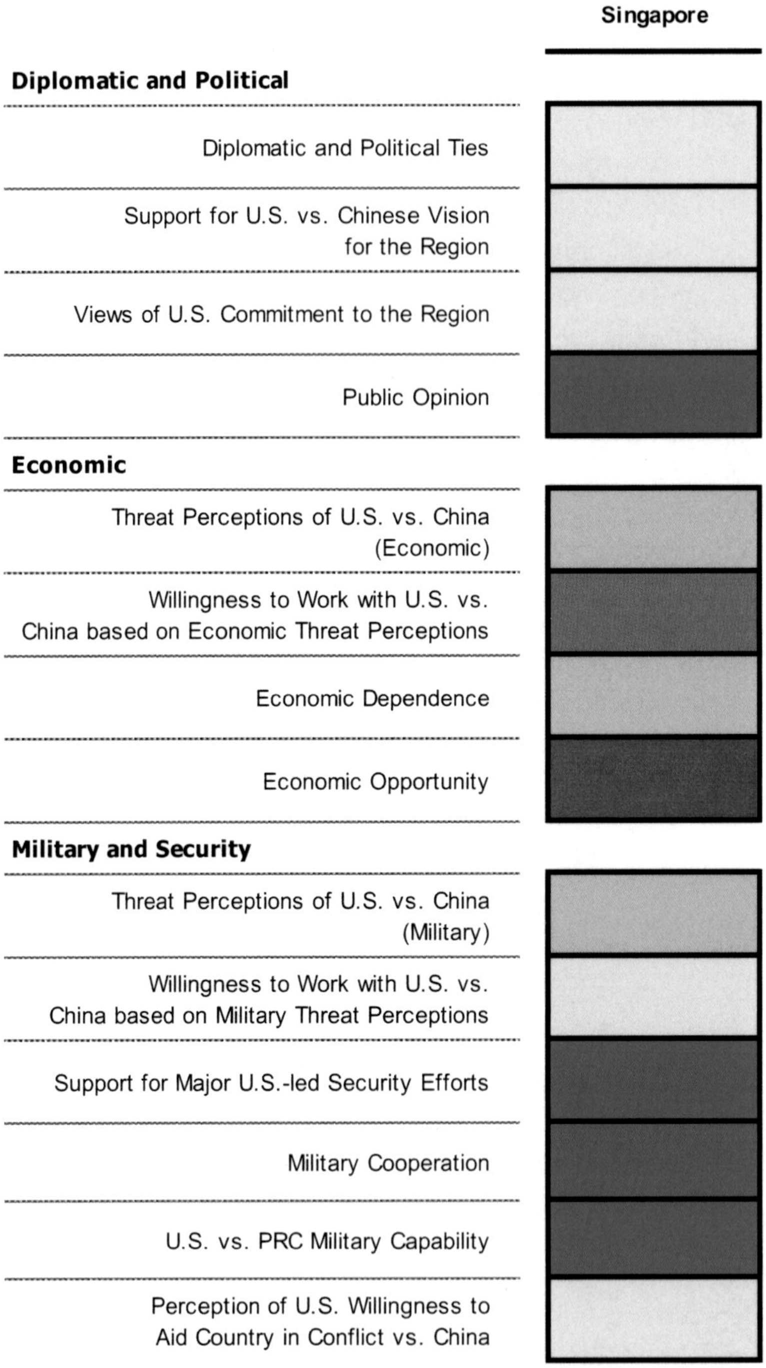

The study includes four quantitative variables for influence: public opinion, economic dependence, military cooperation, and support for U.S. security initiatives. To code public opinion, the research team drew from Pew Research Center, ISEAS–Yusof Ishak Institute, and available regional polls and used interviews to understand public opinion, particularly when there were discrepancies in the polling data. For economic dependence, we collected trade data from United Nations (UN) Comtrade data and foreign direct investment (FDI) and tourism data from the UN, the United States, China, and Singapore. For trade, we examined Singapore's reliance on total trade (imports and exports) with the United States compared with total trade with China.

The research team coded military cooperation according to partner military activities and agreements. This variable aggregates six measures:

1. the presence of U.S. and/or Chinese military basing or facilities
2. relative U.S. versus Chinese arms sales
3. acquisition and cross-servicing agreements
4. defense coproduction and codevelopment agreements
5. information-sharing agreements
6. the quantity and quality of military exercises between Singapore and the United States or China.

The final quantitative variable measures Singaporean support for or opposition to major U.S. security initiatives or efforts. It includes support (or lack thereof) for major U.S. efforts related to North Korea, including efforts to disrupt North Korean ship-to-ship transfers; participation in South China Sea (SCS) patrols, operations, or major exercises with the United States in SCS international waters; engagement in Taiwan Strait transits; support for U.S. freedom of navigation operations; participation in major U.S.-led military operations; and participation in coalition efforts to defeat the Islamic State in Iraq and Syria (ISIS).

As illustrated in Figure 1.1, the United States retains the advantage in the competition for diplomatic influence with Singapore. It also shows greater support for the U.S. vision for the region than for the Chinese vision. However, our research suggests that maintaining U.S. competitive advantage in Singapore will face significant hurdles in the coming decade, particularly as an increasingly competitive U.S.-China relationship has the potential to undermine Singaporean economic growth and stability. The U.S.-Singapore relationship is a success story: Singapore has been and remains a dependable partner for U.S. diplomacy and security efforts in Southeast Asia and the Indo-Pacific region more broadly. Singapore provides operational and logistical support for U.S. forces astride one of the world's most important sea lanes and has punched well above its weight as a diplomatic proponent for rules-based behavior in regional disputes. To sustain this success in ways that will buttress U.S. competitive advantage will require a steady hand at the helm of the relationship, strengthening ties across diplomatic and security domains while recognizing the importance to Singapore of stable relations with and growing ties to China.

Accordingly, Figure 1.1 highlights Chinese advantages in the economic realm. Singapore benefits from a growing trade relationship with China and sees opportunity for investment both in China and in partnerships with China on Belt and Road Initiative (BRI) projects in other countries. Growing trade and investment ties with China could give Beijing coercive leverage, but Singapore views China as more of an economic opportunity than a threat. This view presents challenges to the United States as U.S.-China competition intensifies, particularly if Singapore views the United States as overly aggressive in application of tariffs or punitive actions for countries trading with China. Nonetheless, the United States and many of its allies and partners maintain strong economic relationships with Singapore, especially in terms of FDI.

In regard to military and security variables, Figure 1.1 illustrates U.S. influence in terms of factors such as support for U.S.-led security efforts and defense cooperation. It also indicates that Singapore perceives China as more militarily threatening than the United States in terms of Singaporean security and interests. Singapore maintains much closer security ties with the United States than with China, although recent cooperation between Singapore and Beijing on the security front indicates the importance to Singapore of balance in its security approach. Singapore provides logistics access and infrastructure for U.S. maritime and air forces, basing for regional operations, and mutually beneficial security assistance programs. Sustaining this relationship, and growing it in new areas, is needed to balance against increased Chinese activity and is achievable despite challenges posed by Chinese economic clout and influence operations.

Singapore's position as a very small city-state surrounded by larger, and often unstable, neighbors drives a defense policy and posture based on "twin pillars of deterrence and diplomacy."[2] Singapore's wealth enables the purchase of advanced hardware for the Singapore Armed Forces and for world-class training programs for a largely conscript force of 72,000 active and roughly 350,000 reserve personnel. With what defense analysts consider to be among the best, if not the best, military forces in the region, the Singapore Armed Forces is postured to deter aggression and to participate as a capable partner in military diplomacy and nonwar activities, such as peacekeeping, counterpiracy, and counterterrorism operations. This posture supports a broader strategy of *total defense*, in which every Singaporean is expected to support some aspect of defense in six domains: "military, civil, economic, social, digital, and psychological."[3] In terms of both the total defense strategy and the twin pillars of deterrence and diplomacy, Singapore's security relationship with the United States has been crucial to the accomplishment of its defense objectives. This relationship includes traditional arms sales and training programs, as well as ongoing efforts to strengthen coordination on cyber defenses, biosecurity, and advanced surveillance and reconnaissance capabilities and operations.

An area not separately covered by Figure 1.1 but permeating Singapore's policies and actions across political, economic, and security domains is the influence of sociocultural factors, particularly as they relate to Singapore's majority ethnic Chinese citizenry. The evolution of Singapore's approach to policy decisions impinging on the U.S.-China competition will be shaped to some extent by outcomes related to Chinese influence efforts, which have evolved to conform to the new strategic environment. Chinese efforts that at one time sought to advance the

---

[2] Government of Singapore, Ministry of Defence, "Defence Policy and Diplomacy," webpage, updated March 4, 2019.

[3] Government of Singapore, Ministry of Defence, "Total Defence," webpage, updated February 20, 2020.

ideals of communist revolution in Southeast Asia are now attuned to China's objective to create a larger sphere of influence by associating Chinese ethnic identity with the long-term strategic vision of the Chinese Communist Party.

Singapore's geographic location astride the Straits of Malacca, its outsize influence in the Association of Southeast Asian Nations (ASEAN), and the military support afforded to the United States by infrastructure and access in Singapore, make U.S. investments in its relationship with Singapore a valuable piece of the larger U.S. Indo-Pacific strategy. Singapore's security relationship with the United States and engagement in the region create opportunities for DoD and the USAF to invest resources in both existing and new initiatives. Drawing on a review of government documents, academic articles, media reports, public opinion polls, and interviews with more than 20 senior officials and experts in Singapore and the United States, we explore these issues in the remainder of this report with particular attention to how Singapore is responding to growing strategic competition between the United States and China and how Washington can work together more effectively with Singapore in pursuit of shared diplomatic, economic, and security interests.

Organization of the Report

The remainder of this report is organized as follows:

- In Chapter 2, we review how Singapore's diplomatic relationships with the United States, China, and the other countries in the region are evolving in a more competitive geopolitical environment.
- In Chapter 3, we assess China's economic importance to Singapore and the challenges posed by U.S.-China economic competition, albeit in the context of strong economic ties to the United States and other U.S. allies and partners.
- In Chapter 4, we consider Singapore's defense relationships and priorities in response to growing regional security challenges.
- In Chapter 5, we present an analysis of the outlook in each of these three areas—diplomatic and political, economic, and military and security—over the next five to ten years.
- In Chapter 6, we offer options for the United States and for DoD and the USAF.

2. Singapore's Diplomacy: Maintaining a Delicate Balance

As a small, developed city-state of just over 5.5 million inhabitants, Singapore is dependent on unimpeded access to local trade routes and regional and global markets. Singapore's identity as a major transshipment hub and financial center drives its regional diplomacy and broader foreign policy.[4] In early 2019, Singapore's foreign minister described Singapore's diplomatic strategy as designed to uphold the rules-based global trading system while using Singapore's "soft power" to strengthen partnerships and avoid making enemies.[5] Impartiality and neutrality are underpinning concepts for Singapore's leaders, who view the rise in trade and technology protectionism, identity politics, and "zero-sum" major-power competition as threats to both domestic and regional security.[6] Prime Minister Lee Hsien Loong highlighted these concerns in his opening speech at the 2019 Shangri-La Dialogue, in which he characterized the view from Singapore and Southeast Asia as follows:

> Our world is at a turning point. Globalization is under siege. Tensions between the U.S. and China are growing. Like everyone else, we in Singapore are anxious. We wonder what the future holds, and how countries can collectively find a way forward to maintain peace and prosperity in the world.[7]

However, the key features of Singapore's foreign policy remain relatively constant even in the context of a more tumultuous international situation.

Singapore Prioritizes Sustaining Its Relationship with the United States

The foundation of Singapore's relationship with the United States is anchored by shared interest in "safeguard[ing] the peace, stability and prosperity of the region" that dates to the United States' formal recognition of Singapore in 1966, one year after Singapore gained independence.[8] This shared interest is reflected most clearly in the US-Singapore Free Trade Agreement, signed in 2004 and the first such agreement between the United States and an Asian country. U.S. goods and services trade with Singapore stood at US$90 billion in 2018, with the

---

4 Ankit Panda, "Singapore: A Small Asian Heavyweight," Council on Foreign Relations, June 26, 2018.

5 Linette Lai, "Parliament: Vivian Outlines Foreign Policy Challenges Singapore Faces and How It Will Overcome Them," *Straits Times*, March 1, 2019.

6 Lai, 2019.

7 Government of Singapore, Prime Minister's Office, "PM Lee Hsien Loong at the IISS Shangri-La Dialogue 2019," May 31, 2019.

8 Reaffirming Singapore's Strategic Partnership with the United States, Encompassing Broad and Robust Economic, Military-to-Military, Law Enforcement, and Counterterrorism Cooperation, H.R. Res. 374, 114th Congress, July 12, 2016. Hereafter referred to as H.R. Res. 374, 2016.

United States running a trade surplus of US$18.2 billion.[9] The U.S.-Singapore Third Country Training Programme, established in 2012 and renewed in 2015 to provide joint development assistance to Southeast Asia nations in a variety of areas, is recognized by both parties as a model for bilateral cooperation.[10]

On the defense front, the United States gained access to Singaporean military facilities under a memorandum of understanding signed in 1990, and Singapore became a "Major Security Cooperation Partner" under a strategic framework agreement signed in 2005. In 2014, Singapore became the first Southeast Asian nation to join the Global Coalition to Counter ISIL [the Islamic State of Iraq and the Levant], contributing an aerial refueling tanker, imagery analysis teams, and liaison officers.[11] Singapore also uses its position in ASEAN to advance cooperation: At a U.S.-ASEAN summit held in 2016, Singapore agreed to host a U.S.-ASEAN Connect Center to facilitate cooperation on energy, innovation, and entrepreneurship.

The United States is an indispensable partner for Singapore, and the partnership is at the center of Singapore's approach to national defense. Leaders in Singapore generally share views that are in close alignment with the United States on the importance of maintaining a rules-based order in the region and globally. Diplomatic, economic, and security ties remain very strong overall and are bolstered by shared interests and values. Singapore wants and expects the United States to remain engaged in the region. Analysis of regional polling as recent as 2019 highlights America's enduring importance to Singapore but it also reflects growing concerns about U.S. reliability and predictability.[12] Indeed, there are growing concerns about the sustainability of U.S. leadership and engagement. Such concerns were present during the period of the U.S. "rebalance" to Asia, when many analysts in the region expressed doubts about the sustainability of the U.S. position, given budget constraints and the potential for security problems in other parts of the world to distract U.S. attention, but they have been exacerbated more recently by the U.S. economic agenda and aspects of its foreign policy approach.[13]

Singapore's Prime Minister Lee warned in 2016 that withdrawal from the Trans-Pacific Partnership (TPP) would be a huge blow to U.S. credibility, and analysts in Singapore view the U.S. withdrawal from the TPP as one of several recent strategic missteps on the part of the United States. In addition to U.S. abandonment of the TPP, Singaporean observers are also concerned by the U.S. withdrawal from the Paris Climate Agreement, the Iran nuclear deal, and

---

[9] Office of the United States Trade Representative, "Singapore," webpage, undated.

[10] See H.R. Res. 374, 2016; and Prashanth Parameswaran, "Strengthening US-Singapore Strategic Partnership: Opportunities and Challenges," *RSIS Commentary*, August 8, 2016.

[11] See H.R. Res. 374, 2016.

[12] See Tang Siew Mun, Moe Thuzar, Hoang Thi Ha, Termsak Chalermpalanupap, Pham Thi Phuong Thao, and Anuthida Saelaow Qian, *The State of Southeast Asia: 2019 Survey Report*, Singapore: ISEAS–Yusof Ishak Institute, 2019; and "Asia Loses Confidence in US Leadership," *Asia Sentinel*, June 4, 2019.

[13] Interviews with Singaporean foreign policy experts, Singapore, April 2019.

the Intermediate-Range Nuclear Forces Treaty. In the view of Singaporean officials, a rules-based order requires consistent adherence to established rules.[14] Although the security dimension of the partnership remains very strong, one interviewee noted that this has to be put into the context of the broader competition, stating that "the Chinese Communist Party is focused on politics and influence; the U.S. is focused on military-to-military ties."[15]

Despite concerns with recent U.S. actions in the region, Singapore has even greater fears regarding Chinese regional dominance than some of the other actors in Southeast Asia. They therefore see the United States as an essential foil and hedge. A manageable level of friction between the United States and China puts Singapore in a relatively good position, with the United States providing the security essential to the open trade and shipment lanes that keep Singapore afloat and China providing numerous economic opportunities. Singapore historically judges that the United States values Southeast Asian stability and that Washington is committed to maintaining the U.S.-Singapore partnership. Particularly prior to the current administration, Singapore saw opportunity and success in strengthening U.S. commitment to the region by serving as a hub for U.S. economic engagement in Southeast Asia and embraced the idea of the U.S. rebalance to Asia, even if that contributed to some friction with China. These views generally carry over to the present, but they are being challenged as Singapore deals with a more volatile United States that threatens to cause major economic upheaval via a trade war and heightened tension with China, giving rise to concerns about potential ultimatums that could force "no-win" decisions from smaller regional actors.

Singapore Aims to Reduce Friction in Expanding Relations with China

Since Singapore gained independence in 1965, its relationship with the PRC has more often than not been rocky, but Singapore seeks stable and cooperative ties with China even as demographic concerns and related issues of Chinese influence in Singapore reflect growing concern about China's longer-term objectives.

China-Singapore trade existed even in the absence of formal diplomatic ties for several decades. Bilateral trade stood at S$800 million in the early 1970s, when the relationship first began to blossom (S$1.00 is approximately US$0.70). Reciprocal visits by Lee Kuan Yew to China and Deng Xiaoping to Singapore in the 1970s cemented a cordial relationship and laid the foundation for future formal ties. Deng was impressed by Lee's economic accomplishments under a firm one-party rule.[16] When relations were formalized in 1990, bilateral trade stood at S$5.2 billion. In 2013, China overtook Malaysia as Singapore's largest trade partner; by 2016,

---

[14] Interview with a Singaporean defense official, Singapore, April 2019.

[15] Interview with a Singaporean defense official, Singapore, April 2019.

[16] Lye Liang Fook, "Singapore–China Relations: Building Substantive Ties Amidst Challenges," *Southeast Asian Affairs*, 2018, p. 324.

trade had increased to S$117.2 billion.[17] China has become an increasingly important factor in Singapore's foreign and economic policy over the past decade. Three major intergovernmental projects are evidence of deepening ties in areas of mutual interest. Suzhou Industrial Park represents Singapore's efforts to expand its acumen overseas: specifically, to plan, execute, and administer a major commercial center. The Chongqing Connectivity Initiative is focused on developing business networks in key sectors such as communications, transportation, and logistics. This is part of one of three stated Chinese development strategies: the BRI, Western Region Development, and Yangtze River Economic Belt.[18] The third government-to-government project is the Tianjin Eco-City project. Each of these is overseen by a high-level bilateral joint steering council led by deputy prime minister–level officials on both sides.[19]

However, China's growing influence, military power, and assertive pursuit of its interests are of growing concern in Singapore. Analysts and officials judge that how China uses its growing power over the coming decades will have major implications for the region. As a small state, Singapore has promoted the principle of the protection of rule of law for small states, while China has been less than subtle in pointing out the deference it considers to be owed to larger powers from smaller states. China has bristled at Singapore's past references to the importance of "balance" in regional relationships, indicating that Singapore is siding with the United States in supporting U.S. "rebalancing" to address China's increased influence and power. Singapore has also raised Beijing's ire by criticizing Chinese island-building and construction of military facilities in the SCS.[20]

There are three general areas of discord in Singapore-PRC relations: (1) Singapore-U.S. security cooperation, (2) Singapore military training on Taiwan, and (3) Singapore's support for the 2016 tribunal verdict against China in the case brought by the Philippines regarding Chinese claims and actions in the SCS. Singapore-China relations hit a low point that year when Singaporean diplomats accused China of attempting to divide ASEAN after China's foreign minister announced that China had reached a consensus on the SCS with Brunei, Laos, and Cambodia. Several other disagreements ensued related to ASEAN-China relations and the SCS issue; in November 2016, Hong Kong Customs seized nine Singaporean Terrex infantry transport vehicles transiting a Hong Kong container terminal while returning from a training exercise in Taiwan.[21] The issue of the Terrex vehicles illustrated concerns about how China could use various forms of leverage to pressure Singapore, and these concerns became more

---

[17] Fook, 2018, p. 326.

[18] Fook, 2018, p. 332.

[19] Fook, 2018, p. 322.

[20] Fook, 2018, pp. 333–335.

[21] Fook, 2018, p. 333.

visible as relations with China went through a downturn, with Beijing expressing displeasure on several other fronts as well.[22]

Singapore-China relations have nevertheless rebounded. In early 2017, the two countries resumed the suspended Joint Council for Bilateral Cooperation Meeting that oversees the three government-to-government projects.[23] Additionally, some of Singapore's concerns about points of friction in its relationship with China are offset by short-term realities: As of this writing, Singapore's economic performance is sluggish, and national elections in 2020 marked a transition to a new generation of leaders. Given these considerations, Singapore is undertaking an effort to boost its ties with Beijing.[24]

Singapore Expands Its Engagement with Other Countries in the Region

Singapore prioritizes improving its ties with other countries in Southeast Asia and beyond. Much of this effort centers on its role in ASEAN. In addition to further ASEAN integration and closer ties with ASEAN member countries, Singapore is pursuing expanded ties with other countries in the Indo-Pacific region (most notably, Australia, India, and Japan). Singapore's deep connectivity and influence in the web of regional U.S. allies and partners reinforces its value to the United States in considering regional programs and initiatives. Having Singapore as a stakeholder in the consultation and implementation of regional policy actions increases the likelihood of larger regional buy-in.

Key to Singapore's approach to foreign relations is its position in ASEAN. Singapore was a founding member of ASEAN in 1967 and remains an influential partner for both the United States and China within that body, particularly in terms of advancing interests in ASEAN-led forums, such as the East Asia Summit, ASEAN Regional Forum, and the ASEAN Defence Ministers' Meeting Plus. ASEAN matters a great deal to Singapore: It views the organization as the primary way for small states (including itself) to "tie in" larger powers so that the interests of the small states remain relevant.[25] Singapore had a particularly delicate balancing act in its role as the country coordinator for ASEAN-China dialogue (which it held for three years until 2018). SCS issues and the major-power politics and posturing associated with them are front and center

---

[22] The authors thank Prashanth Parameswaran for raising this point.

[23] Fook, 2018, p. 335.

[24] The authors thank Prashanth Parameswaran for raising this point.

[25] It is worth noting that there is an alternate view held by some in the region that Singapore's founder Lee Kuan Yew and some of the country's leading diplomats have been more cautious in their embrace of ASEAN, rather than its strongest supporters. Some former and current officials are still focused on managing expectations for ASEAN, and they are sometimes quite candid about its challenges and limitations geopolitically. The authors thank Prashanth Parameswaran for raising this point.

as Singapore performs this role while ASEAN and China attempt to broker a code of conduct for the SCS.[26]

ASEAN's strengths and shortcomings, therefore, become Singapore's. One regional expert noted that "Singapore can't admit that ASEAN is weak but knows that ASEAN can't really formulate an effective 'Indo-Pacific Strategy' of its own or even a coordinated response to the U.S. strategy."[27] Singapore is also concerned about regional multilateral forums that it believes might draw influence away from ASEAN or exacerbate tensions with China. According to interviewees, the U.S. Free and Open Indo-Pacific (FOIP) concept is not emphatically embraced by Singapore because it could challenge "ASEAN centrality" if it embraces or creates alternative forums. Beyond concerns about what it might mean for ASEAN centrality, Singapore has other concerns about the U.S. FOIP concept. Some Singaporean officials, including Foreign Minister Vivian Balakrishnan, have expressed reservations about the way the U.S. FOIP concept has evolved and have noted that Singapore's vision for a regional concept focuses on the need for greater inclusivity and a stronger emphasis on economics.[28] Such comments appear to reflect officials' concerns about certain aspects of U.S. policy under the Trump administration, particularly with respect to free trade and multilateralism.[29]

The U.S. FOIP concept also could exacerbate intensified competition between the United States and China, increasing the likelihood of armed conflict at flashpoints such as the SCS.[30] For example, should the U.S.-Australia-India-Japan Quadrilateral Dialogue (the Quad) become a FOIP cornerstone in the security realm, the importance of ASEAN-led security dialogue could be called into question, and China's likely response to containment actions by the Quad would further constrain the ability of smaller powers to manage stable relations with the PRC.[31] Quad dialogue and objectives thus far, however, indicate that this sensitivity is understood by the respective parties: At the Quad meeting in Bangkok in May 2019, participants reaffirmed ASEAN centrality while avoiding specific security initiatives that might prompt escalatory Chinese behavior.[32]

Singapore has prioritized ensuring the success of ASEAN. According to Singapore's Ministry of Foreign Affairs, "As a small nation-state, Singapore strongly supports ASEAN's

---

[26] Parameswaran, 2016.

[27] Interview with a Singaporean academic and foreign policy expert, Singapore, April 2019.

[28] Vivian Balakrishnan, "MFA Press Release: Speech by Minister for Foreign Affairs Dr Vivian Balakrishnan During the Committee of Supply Debate, 1 March 2018," Singapore: Ministry of Foreign Affairs, March 1, 2018.

[29] Some of these debates surfaced in Singapore's approach to the ASEAN "Outlook on the Indo-Pacific" adopted by ASEAN in early 2020. The authors thank Prashanth Parameswaran for raising this point.

[30] Interview with a Singaporean academic and foreign policy expert, Singapore, April 2019.

[31] Interviews with Southeast Asian security policy experts, Singapore, April 2019.

[32] Patrick M. Cronin, "US Asia Strategy: Beyond the Quad," *The Diplomat*, March 9, 2019.

goal of building a strong, prosperous and rules-based ASEAN."[33] Singapore is closely engaged with ASEAN-led platforms, including the ASEAN Plus Three, East Asia Summit, ASEAN Regional Forum, and ASEAN Defence Ministers' Meeting Plus. Singapore is also an active participant in ASEAN Dialogue Partnerships, and Singapore is currently serving as the coordinator for ASEAN–European Union dialogue (from 2018 to 2021). Singapore has also emphasized strengthening its bilateral ties with other ASEAN member countries: Brunei, Cambodia, Indonesia, Laos, Malaysia, Myanmar, the Philippines, Thailand, and Vietnam. In particular, Singapore enjoys a growing relationship with Indonesia, which includes an annual leaders' retreat, regular high-level exchanges, economic working group meetings, and cooperation in areas such as education, culture, defense, and the environment. Singapore and Indonesia also have an increasingly important economic relationship, and Singapore became Indonesia's largest source of FDI in 2014.

Looking beyond Southeast Asia, Singapore is strengthening its relationship with Australia. The two countries have a close, long-standing relationship and signed a Comprehensive Strategic Partnership in 2015. The Comprehensive Strategic Partnership expands cooperation in four key areas:

1. economics, trade, and investment
2. foreign affairs, defense, and security
3. science and innovation
4. people-to-people exchanges.[34]

The following year, in 2016, the two countries announced a series of initiatives to strengthen cooperation in each of these four areas.[35] Singapore and Australia also have a strong economic partnership, as reflected by the 2003 Singapore-Australia Free Trade Agreement, which was updated in 2017.[36] The two countries are also part of the ASEAN-Australia-New Zealand Free Trade Agreement and the Comprehensive and Progressive Agreement for Trans-Pacific Partnership (CPTPP).[37] Additionally, Singapore and Australia enjoy close defense ties. The two countries are members of the Five Power Defense Arrangements, and Singapore's armed forces train in Australia (as detailed further in Chapter 4).

Another priority for Singaporean diplomacy is expanding its engagement with India. The two countries signed the India-Singapore Strategic Partnership when Prime Minister Narendra Modi

---

[33] Government of Singapore, Ministry of Foreign Affairs, "ASEAN," webpage, undated a.

[34] Prashanth Parameswaran, "Australia and Singapore: What's in a New Strategic Partnership?" *The Diplomat*, June 30, 2015.

[35] Government of Singapore, Ministry of Foreign Affairs, "MFA Press Statement: Singapore-Australia Comprehensive Strategic Partnership Package," press release, May 6, 2016.

[36] Australian Government, Department of Foreign Affairs and Trade, "Singapore-Australia FTA," webpage, undated b.

[37] Australian Government, Department of Foreign Affairs and Trade, "ASEAN-Australia-New Zealand FTA," webpage, undated a.

visited Singapore in November 2015, and it was updated to include financial technology and innovation during Prime Minister Modi's May–June 2018 visit.[38] India is an important economic partner for Singapore, as underscored by the Comprehensive Economic Cooperation Agreement the two countries signed in 2005.[39] Singapore is among India's top sources of FDI. Although economic ties constitute an important part of the relationship, the two countries also hold regular exchanges on foreign policy and security issues. Singapore maintains two ministerial dialogues with India, the Foreign Ministers' Joint Ministerial Committee for Bilateral Cooperation and the India-Singapore Defence Ministers' Dialogue, reflecting the importance of the bilateral relationship in the areas of foreign policy and defense affairs.[40]

Singapore is also working to strengthen its relationship with Japan. The Singapore-Japan relationship centers on regular high-level exchanges, close economic ties, and cooperation in areas such as defense, counterproliferation, export controls, environment, biomedical research, and cybersecurity. According to Singapore's Ministry of Foreign Affairs, the two countries

> share many common interests on regional and international issues and collaborate closely under Singapore's largest and most successful joint training programme with another country—the Japan-Singapore Partnership Programme for the 21st Century (JSPP21)—to provide technical assistance to third countries.[41]

The work plan for JSPP21 focuses on providing training courses to government officials—mainly from ASEAN member states, particularly the Mekong countries (Cambodia, Laos, Myanmar, Thailand, and Vietnam)—in areas such as maritime safety management, international law of the sea, urban development, intellectual property protection, disaster risk reduction and management, and financial technology and digital economy.[42]

Beyond Singapore's prioritization of ASEAN and its desire to expand its ties with key countries, other international and domestic developments also affect how Singapore views its regional relationships. Internationally, for example, the election of Philippine President Rodrigo Duterte in 2016 has influenced Singapore's consideration of the SCS issue in the context of its regional ties. From Singapore's perspective, Duterte's downplaying of the SCS dispute, including the tribunal ruling, in his pursuit of warmer ties with China has made it more difficult for Singapore, as a nonclaimant but interested party, to push harder on the SCS issue.[43] Domestically, as the U.S.-China rivalry intensifies, there has been a debate within Singapore about whether it should continue to speak out on geopolitics and maintain an outsize role in

---

[38] Government of Singapore, Ministry of Foreign Affairs, "India," webpage, undated b.

[39] Government of India, Department of Commerce, "Indian Trade Portal," webpage, undated.

[40] Government of Singapore, Ministry of Foreign Affairs, undated b.

[41] Government of Singapore, Ministry of Foreign Affairs, "Japan," webpage, undated c.

[42] Ministry of Foreign Affairs of Japan, "Japan-Singapore Partnership Programme for the 21st Century (JSPP21) Planning Committee Meeting on the FY 2019 Annual Work Plan," press release, May 16, 2019.

[43] The authors thank Prashanth Parameswaran for raising this point.

regional foreign policy issues (as it did under Lee Kuan Yew) or instead adopt a more modest role and a quieter tone in line with its status as a small state. In 2017, this so-called small state debate was illustrated by Kishore Mahbubani's comparison of Singapore to Qatar, which sparked comments by other leading diplomats, such as Bilahari Kausikan, who argued that Singapore should not hesitate to stand up for its interests.[44] Part of the debate was revealed through dueling op-eds in the *Straits Times*. In an op-ed arguing that Singapore should act like a small state, Mahbubani said, "In the jungle, no small animal would stand in front of a charging elephant, no matter who has the right of way, so long as the elephant is not charging over the small animal's home territory."[45] Bilahari published his own op-ed, in which he countered that "Singapore did not survive and prosper by being anybody's tame poodle."[46]

Singapore Views Intensifying U.S.-China Competition as Long on Challenge, Short on Opportunity

Singapore views intensifying U.S.-China competition through two lenses. The first focuses on opportunities provided by increased U.S. economic and diplomatic investment as a response to China's growing clout in the region. The second focuses on the challenges inherent in the potential escalation of tensions, in which either of the two powers might seek to decouple Singapore from the other. Singapore needs transshipment to survive, and anything that restricts Singapore's access to trade routes, or the access of others to Singapore, is particularly threatening. Singaporeans do not want to be forced to choose to live in one of two diametrically opposed ecosystems: They draw sustenance from both. As one interviewee put it, "Singapore's goal is simple: open flow of trade, people, and funds."[47] The most recent (2017) U.S. National Security Strategy is a double-edged sword for Singapore. It provides clear pushback on China (which previous strategies lacked in Singapore's view) but potentially marks a turn by the United States to a full-spectrum competition that will force regional actors to take sides. Singapore wants pushback on China and does not want to do it itself but also seeks diplomatic and economic equilibrium. Polling also reflects the challenges that a more competitive U.S.-China relationship presents and the uncertainty about what this relationship could mean for Singaporean interests in the future.[48]

When marking the end of Singapore's ASEAN Chairmanship in November 2018, Singapore's foreign minister outlined major accomplishments, highlighting two that indicate the

---

[44] See Charissa Yong, "Should Small States Act Like Small States?" *Straits Times*, July 9, 2017.

[45] Kishore Mahbubani, "Qatar: Big Lessons from a Small Country," *Straits Times*, July 1, 2017.

[46] Bilahari Kausikan, "Singapore Cannot Be Cowed by Size," *Straits Times*, July 3, 2017.

[47] Interview with a Singaporean government official, Singapore, April 2019.

[48] See Tang et al., 2019; 79 percent of Singaporean respondents thought that the impact of the U.S.-China trade war was either unclear or bad for Singapore and the regional economy.

importance Singapore places on both ASEAN dialogue with China and maintaining stability through rules-based trading mechanisms and blocs. These two accomplishments were an agreed draft negotiating text for a code of conduct in the SCS and advances on negotiations toward the Regional Comprehensive Economic Partnership (RCEP), a trade agreement that would form the world's largest trading bloc.[49] Should obstacles to RCEP implementation (primarily between India and China) be removed, this would be a major gain for China, further strengthening China's economic links with ASEAN and other regional countries in a bloc that does not include the United States.

As Singapore handed over the ASEAN chairmanship to Thailand at the end of 2018, Singapore Prime Minister Lee Hsien Loong clearly warned that changes were afoot in an environment in which member states do not want to "take sides" in a major-power feud but might be forced to "choose one or the other" side on certain issues.[50] Interlocutors believe that he was strongly messaging the United States about problems associated with regional actors being forced into bad choices: choices in which decisions might not go according to U.S. desires.[51] In this dynamic environment, several interviewees pointed out that U.S. leadership is, at best, not fully attuned to regional trends and, at worst, dismissive of them. As one interview said, "Singapore wants to tell the U.S. what is happening in the region, but is anyone listening?"[52]

Interviewees noted the deleterious impact of differences, real or perceived, between heads of U.S. agencies when they speak about regional commitments and actual policy decisions.[53] As one interviewee stated, "More clarity in U.S. foreign policy would help."[54] The United States is traditionally effective at "rule-of-law" narratives and actions, but interlocutors in Singapore felt this effectiveness has weakened, with talk of a rules-based order lacking credibility in the absence of public diplomacy and outreach efforts.[55]

Singapore needs to have a productive relationship with China and wants a strong partnership with the United States, but the emergence of a more competitive U.S.-China relationship has raised the prospect that Singapore might have to redefine its relationship with the United States,

---

[49] Afifah Ariffin, "ASEAN Chair: Singapore Has Accomplished Far More Than Anticipated," *CNA*, November 11, 2018. For more information on RCEP, see Luke Hunt, "How Close Is RCEP to Reality?" *The Diplomat*, October 16, 2019.

[50] Seow Bei Yi, "ASEAN Has to Work with the World as It Is: PM Lee Hsien Loong," *Straits Times*, November 15, 2018.

[51] Interviews with Asian security and foreign policy experts, Singapore, April 2019.

[52] Interview with a Singaporean expert on U.S. Indo-Pacific policy, Singapore, April 2019. At the time of the interview, the Singaporean expert pointed out that U.S. ambassadorships to both Singapore and ASEAN had been vacant since 2017.

[53] Interview with a Singaporean expert on U.S. Indo-Pacific policy, Singapore, April 2019. The U.S. decision to pull out of military exercises with South Korea was an example given in several discussions with Singaporean and Singapore-based foreign policy experts.

[54] Interview with a third-country academic and foreign policy expert, Singapore, April 2019.

[55] Interviews with a Singaporean government official, Singapore, April 2019.

China, or both.[56] Most interviewees felt that Singapore could weather the storm as it is now, but they are eager to avoid a situation in which the United States and China become not just strategic competitors but fierce adversaries. Aspects of the trade war are understandable to Singapore's business and political elites, but the broader Singapore population views it as "upsetting the apple cart."[57]

Some Singaporean experts point out that, in the economic realm, the United States has largely left the competition to the private sector: One expert questioned whether U.S. leaders really think the private sector will be able to keep up with China and its "whole-of-government" approach.[58] Any imbalance in the competition in China's favor is clearly on the economic side, but Singaporeans do not want the United States to wreck their economy to "fix" the imbalance. The desire is for more U.S. official leadership: Most interviewees noted that the United States passed on a "golden opportunity" to exercise this leadership through the TPP when it withdrew from the agreement in January 2017.[59] The agreement was viewed in Singapore as a clear chance for the United States to promote the rules-based order in Asia, but the United States failed to seize this opportunity and, to date, has not developed a sufficient strategy to economically balance and complement the military presence in the region. The Asia Reassurance Initiative Act passed by the U.S. Congress at the end of 2018 provides a show of bipartisan commitment, and investment of money, by Congress, but the proof for regionally focused leaders in Singapore will be in the details.

Singaporean experts also generally believe that U.S. officials and strategists do not fully understand China's BRI, overlooking domestic Chinese drivers of the initiative and overstating the degree of harm most BRI projects might generate.[60] Singapore does not need BRI infrastructure development but does see ample opportunity to benefit by assisting China in financing BRI projects through the Asia Infrastructure Investment Bank (AIIB), and several Singaporean companies provide other BRI-related services. Apart from the BRI, Singapore's investment within China is large and growing: In many ways, it is as important to Singapore as FDI coming into the city-state from the United States and other sources. The importance of trade with China justifiably draws attention as a lever of influence, but it is not the only factor in play.

On the security side, most Singaporeans are happy, if quietly so, with what the United States is doing and feel that the relationship is balanced. Singapore is willing to send strong signals of its commitment to the security relationship. For example, Singapore in 2015 made the decision to

---

[56] Interview with a Singaporean academic and foreign policy expert, Singapore, April 2019. See also Glen Carey and Philip Heijmans, "Singapore Urges U.S. to Accept China as Competitor," *Bloomberg*, May 17, 2019.

[57] Interview with a Singaporean academic and economist, Singapore, April 2019.

[58] Interview with a Singaporean academic and economist, Singapore, April 2019.

[59] Interviews with Singapore-based foreign policy experts, Singapore, April 2019.

[60] Interviews with a U.S.-based economist and a Singaporean academic and economist, Los Angeles, March 2019, and Singapore, April 2019.

allow U.S. P-8 reconnaissance flights from its territory at a particularly sensitive time of Chinese activity in the SCS, angering China and offering a counterpoint to its neighbor Malaysia's wavering support for such operations.[61] Several interviewees noted that as long as the United States intends to stay in the region and not force zero-sum choices, the level of U.S.-Singapore security cooperation can grow in several areas related to advanced defense technologies, arms sales, and nontraditional security cooperation areas, such as cyber. The context is important: A zero-sum game between the United States and China will mean that all security actions could lead to misunderstandings and constrain expanded cooperation.[62]

There are no signs that Singapore will retreat even a little from being the United States' most important security partner in Southeast Asia, but this partnership must be reevaluated on a much more frequent basis because of China's intensifying efforts to undermine regional support for U.S. security relationships and activities—which are subject to greater uncertainty as well. As one discussant put it, "The U.S. is increasingly a question mark, and China increasingly an exclamation point."[63] Singapore's Ministry of Defence is institutionally tied to the United States in very concrete ways, but interviewees indicated that its agencies and leaders are beginning to grapple with the question "what if we have to choose?" Whether and how Singapore adjusts to this reality will be seen in specific areas of Singaporean contribution to U.S. access and situational awareness.[64]

The SCS issue illustrates the complex nature of the challenge facing Singapore in navigating the increasingly competitive regional security environment. Although Singapore is not a claimant to any SCS features, SCS contention features prominently in its management of relations with the United States, China, and its ASEAN neighbors. Interviewees noted three SCS narratives that are at work as Singapore's leaders grapple with SCS pressures and fallout. The first is a PRC-driven narrative that plays into Singapore's official desires for dispute settlement, which says that tensions are decreasing, and China and ASEAN are working out issues via code of conduct negotiations. Singapore wants this to be true but recognizes that China pushes this narrative largely to portray the United States as an outsider causing instability, which runs contrary to Singapore's desire for the United States to maintain a security presence in the SCS. The second narrative posits that China has already sealed control of the SCS, and ASEAN states and the United States must find a way to accept that fact and save face as best they can under the circumstances. This is largely unacceptable to Singapore's leadership because it promotes the inevitability of Chinese regional dominance and commensurate pressure on Singapore to accept

[61] See "China Military Paying 'Close Attention' to US Plane Deployment in Singapore," *Straits Times*, December 9, 2015.

[62] Interviews with Singapore-based international security experts, Singapore, April 2019.

[63] Interview with a Southeast Asian security expert, Singapore, April 2019.

[64] Interviews with Singaporean defense officials, Singapore, April 2019.

China's reinterpretation of norms and rules.[65] The last narrative, probably the most distasteful to Singapore, says that the United States and China are bound to come to blows as the competition heats up, and the SCS is an obvious stage for the showdown.[66]

In sum, Singaporean analysts and officials are keenly aware of the increasingly competitive nature of the U.S.-China relationship. They assess that growing competition in the U.S.-China relationship has the potential to create problems for Singapore's economy and to exacerbate the dilemmas Singapore faces in some of its key relationships. Additionally, there are concerns about how a more competitive U.S.-China relationship could play out in other parts of the region that are important to Singapore's interests: notably, in Southeast Asia, where analysts note that countries want to avoid making a choice between the United States and China.

The Domestic Political Landscape: Identity and Chinese Influence

Singapore's regional outlook and responses to changes in the geostrategic environment are also driven by its distinct domestic polity and demography. The challenges associated with Singapore's responses to an increasingly competitive international landscape are exacerbated by the city-state's internal political environment. As pressure mounts from both China and the United States for Singapore to align with specific, increasingly opposed positions, Singapore prepares for a general election (due before 2021) that will either bring a new generation of leadership from the ruling People's Action Party, in power since the country's founding, or see a major shift in the evolution of democracy in Singapore if an opposition party or coalition prevails.[67] The next general election will be an important period for Singapore's electorate to sway next-generation leaders as they formulate responses to an increasingly competitive environment.

Singapore's citizenry is majority ethnic Chinese (76 percent), with Malay (15 percent) and Indian (7 percent) ethnic groups comprising the remainder. The government hopes to maintain about 75 percent of the population as ethnic Chinese, but low birth rates in this group mean that Chinese must come from elsewhere to sustain this representation. Efforts by Singapore's leaders to maintain the current ethnic percentages have underpinned the flow of mainland Chinese into Singapore, but these efforts raise concern about how China might increasingly leverage political,

---

[65] Interviews with Singaporean security and economic experts pointed out fears that increasing Chinese power, if unchecked by the United States, would allow Beijing to pursue unfair trade and investment policies that would overwhelm the interests of smaller states and to force acceptance of Beijing's definitions of territorial sovereignty and extension of exclusive economic zone rights in the SCS, to the detriment of counterclaimants with whom Singapore coordinates on rule-of-law and regional stability policies.

[66] Interview with a Singaporean defense expert, Singapore, April 2019.

[67] Kristen Han, "The Guessing Game for Singapore's Elections," *The Interpreter*, July 16, 2019.

economic, and security decisions, which Singapore has worked hard to avoid.[68] Although such efforts have not (to this point) resulted in a noticeable trend of political support among the populace for pro-PRC positions, they open potential avenues for Chinese influence operations in the coming years.[69]

The evolution of Singapore's approach to policy decisions that affect U.S.-China competition will be shaped to some extent by outcomes related to Chinese influence efforts. Chinese attempts to influence Singapore are not new, but they have evolved to conform to the new strategic environment. Efforts that at one time sought to advance the ideals of communist revolution to Southeast Asia are now attuned to Chinese objectives to create a larger sphere of influence by associating Chinese ethnic identity with the long-term strategic objectives of the Chinese Communist Party. Many of China's ethnic Chinese citizens belong to clan and temple associations, business groups, or other cultural organizations based on Chinese ethnic identity. These entities are targeted by Chinese United Front activities intended to promote the idea of a "greater China" that should be supported by ethnic Chinese loyalty, regardless of location and citizenship.[70] There are parallels with Chinese United Front efforts in Taiwan and Hong Kong in terms of how the PRC uses temple associations and clan networks to disseminate propaganda.

Cultural exchanges between China and Singapore are deep and varied. The China Cultural Center opened in Singapore in 2015 during a state visit by Chinese leader Xi Jinping to Singapore: the first such center in the world.[71] China also seeks to influence Singaporean elite thinking via paid trips for academics and other thought leaders.[72] China pushes the idea that Chinese culture must be tied to the PRC politically, and several interviewees indicated that there are an increasing number of people in Singapore who buy the Chinese narrative. Data breaches in Singapore are broad because information is not compartmentalized in most official Singaporean databases, providing numerous weak points for China to exploit as it looks at targets for United Front activities.[73]

Media and public opinion must also be considered, given the potential to influence Singapore's politics and policy. Interviewees noted that Singapore media continues to feature Southeast Asia coverage but also is increasingly home to stories and editorials pushing narratives associated with "greater China" ideas.[74] Singapore cable television packages increasingly offer

---

[68] See Andrew Jacobs, "In Singapore, Vitriol Against Chinese Newcomers," *New York Times*, July 26, 2012; and Amy Qin, "Worries Grow over China's Calls to Help 'Motherland,'" *New York Times*, August 5, 2018.

[69] Russell Hsiao, "A Preliminary Survey of CCP Influence Operations in Singapore," *China Brief*, July 16, 2019.

[70] Hsiao, 2019.

[71] Fook, 2018, p. 331.

[72] See Hsiao, 2019, and Qin, 2018.

[73] Interview with a Singaporean academic and media expert, Singapore, April 2019.

[74] Interview with a Singaporean academic and media expert, Singapore, April 2019.

networks that have shifted to pro-PRC channels, particularly by offering Hong Kong and Taiwan channels that have been bought out by PRC interests.

Singapore's leaders seek to keep demographics from creating sociopolitical fissures by maintaining the current ethnic makeup of the population and reinforcing through government sponsored campaigns the "unique" nature of Singaporean identity.[75] Singapore has worked assiduously to establish a Singaporean identity that eschews ethnic nativism among its Chinese, Malay, and Indian citizens. Singapore's leaders do not openly express fear of mainland Chinese sympathies among new arrivals, but several interviewees indicated that such concerns are increasing in private.[76] One interviewee noted that Singapore exercises a "passive-aggressive" approach to PRC influence efforts, conveying messages back to Beijing that make it seem like Singaporeans are not worried about Chinese activities, while they are in fact a source of growing concern.[77]

---

[75] See for example Lee Hsien Loong, "Commentary: From Singapore to Singaporeans, the Making of a National Identity," *CNA*, August 19, 2019a.

[76] Interviews with Singaporean and third-country, Singapore-based public policy experts, Singapore, April 2019.

[77] Interview with a Singaporean academic and media expert, Singapore, April 2019.

3. China's Economic Importance to Singapore

China Is the Largest Trade Partner and Export Destination for Singapore

China has been Singapore's largest trading partner since 2013. China is also the leading destination for Singapore's exports. The China-Singapore Free Trade Agreement that entered into force in January 2009 was upgraded in November 2018. Singapore's Ministry of Foreign Affairs characterizes the upgraded China-Singapore Free Trade Agreement as offering improved market access for Singapore's goods and services exports to China and greater transparency and predictability for business activities.[78] Singapore was also an early supporter of the BRI and signed a memorandum of understanding in 2014, along with several other countries, to establish the AIIB. The AIIB is key to financing several BRI projects, and Singapore's participation lends financial strength to BRI lending. Singapore is not a major recipient of BRI project work but can provide financial and legal support and other services in managing projects. The Singapore Business Federation and China Enterprises Association jointly launched the BRI Connect Platform in 2017 to provide members with a means to

> share information on the latest developments on the BRI, provide market analysis and intelligence, conduct feasibility and evaluation services, assist in project investment and financing, offer legal and arbitration consultation, set up online and offline BRI project-matching activities, promote the development of talent capability and showcase successful BRI stories.[79]

Singapore has less of a concern about China as an economic threat than some countries that were examined as part of this project, quite simply because Singapore sees China as a huge economic opportunity, both as a destination for Singaporean investment and as a partner in need of Singaporean expertise and support for broader regional efforts, such as the BRI, AIIB, and RCEP. Because of its wealth and service sector expertise, Singapore has less to fear than its less developed neighbors from Chinese economic leverage or debt entrapment: The greater threat to Singapore would come from an escalating trade war or, worse still, from Chinese economic collapse or catastrophe.

The United States Remains Singapore's Leading Source of Foreign Direct Investment

In contrast to China's importance as Singapore's trade partner, particularly as Singapore's top export market, the United States is the largest investor in Singapore. As of the end of 2017,

---

[78] Government of Singapore, Ministry of Foreign Affairs, "People's Republic of China," webpage, undated d.

[79] Fook, 2018, p. 331.

U.S. investment accounted for more than 21 percent of foreign investment in Singapore. China figures less prominently in terms of foreign investment, accounting for only 3.5 percent as of the end of 2017.

Table 3.1 combines trade and FDI data to show that although China may be the single most important bilateral economic trade partner for Singapore, China's economic influence decreases when combining the economic influence that the United States and other allies and partners could wield.

Table 3.1. Combined Trade and Foreign Direct Investment Data

Country	Percentage of Total Singaporean Trade (2018)	Percentage of Total FDI Stock in Singapore (2017)
China (mainland, Macau, and Hong Kong)	20%	3%
United States	9%	21%
United States, Australia, and Japan	17%	

SOURCES: United Nations, "UN Comtrade Database," webpage, undated; U.S. Bureau of Economic Analysis, "Direct Investment by Country and Industry," webpage, updated July 24, 2019; American Enterprise Institute and Heritage Foundation, China Global Investment Tracker, homepage, undated; International Monetary Fund, "World Economic Outlook Database October 2018," October 9, 2018; Transparency International, "Corruption Perceptions Index: 2018," webpage, 2018; People's Republic of China, Ministry of Commerce, *2017 Statistical Bulletin of China's Outward Foreign Direct Investment*, October 2018.
NOTE: 2017 figures were used for FDI data, and 2018 figures were used for trade. Unless otherwise specified, dollar values are expressed in current U.S. dollars of the year to which they refer.

It is important to note, however, that China has been Singapore's top investment destination since 1997. In 2015, Singapore's investment in China reached US$121 billion.[80] Singapore has been China's largest investor since 2013, a fact that is a key determinant of the overall health of several Singapore businesses.

Other Potential Economic Levers, Such as Chinese Tourism and Students

Another set of economic concerns that has emerged over the past decade centers on possible Chinese attempts to use economic leverage to coerce Singapore in response to disputes over other issues. Chinese tourism is one such potential source of leverage. Despite rocky relations in 2016, Chinese tourists to Singapore hit a record 2.86 million—a close second to Indonesian tourists at 2.89 million. In 2017, Chinese tourists exceeded those of Indonesia to top the list. In 2018, Chinese tourists constituted 18.4 percent of all tourists to Singapore, significantly more than U.S. tourists (3.5 percent) .[81] This influx is accompanied by a large and growing number of

[80] Fook, 2018, p. 326.

[81] Government of Singapore, Singapore Tourism Board, "International Visitor Arrivals," webpage, undated.

Chinese students (almost 5,000 Chinese exchange students in 2016) pursuing educational opportunities in Singapore. [82]

[82] Center for Strategic and International Studies, China Power Project, "Is China Both a Source and Hub for International Students?" webpage, undated.

4. Singapore Defense Relations: Heavily Favoring United States but Not Snubbing China

In this chapter, we look at how Singapore's defense relationships with the United States, China, and the region have evolved in response to growing security challenges associated with China's rise and U.S.-China competition. Singapore has been and remains a key security partner for the United States in an important geographical location, providing logistics access and infrastructure for U.S. maritime and air forces, basing for regional operations, and mutually beneficial security assistance programs. Sustaining this relationship, and growing it in new areas, is needed to balance against increased Chinese activity and is achievable despite challenges posed by Chinese economic clout and influence operations.

Singapore Is Strengthening Its Security Partnership with the United States

The United States is Singapore's most important arms supplier, provides essential training facilities for Singapore forces as part of arms sales packages, and cooperates in a variety of counterterrorism, cyber, and maritime security efforts. Singapore hosts a U.S. Navy logistics command element that coordinates regional operations.[83] U.S. Navy littoral combat ships conduct rotational deployments to Singapore's Changi Naval Base.[84] The United States hosts Republic of Singapore Air Force (RSAF) training detachments of F-16C/D fighter jets and Apache helicopters at bases in Arizona and of F-15SG fighters in Idaho.[85] Singapore's pending purchase of U.S. F-35 Joint Strike Fighters will further enhance the relationship and open the door for enhanced interoperability with the United States, Japan, and Australia.[86]

The two sides have had a Strategic Security Policy Dialogue since 2006, and it is highly institutionalized, with the tenth iteration of talks held in April 2019.[87] The United States conducts regular P-8 flights and flights of USAF aircraft out of Singapore bases. More than 100 U.S. Navy

---

[83] H.R. Res. 374, 2016.

[84] Franz-Stefan Gady, "US Navy Littoral Combat Ship Arrives in Singapore for Rotational Deployment," *The Diplomat*, July 9, 2019.

[85] The Peace Carvin II detachment at Luke Air Force Base, Ariz., was established in 1992 and conducts training using the RSAF's F-16C/D Fighting Falcons. The Peace Carvin V detachment at Mountain Home Air Force Base, Idaho, was established in 2008 and conducts training using the RSAF's F-15SG fighters. The Peace Vanguard detachment in Marana, Ariz., was established in 2001 and conducts training using the RSAF's Ah-64 Apache helicopters. See Republic of Singapore Air Force, "Overseas Training and Detachments," webpage, undated.

[86] Jonathan D. Caverly, Ethan B. Kapstein, and Srdjan Vucetic, "F-35 Sales Are America's Belt and Road," *Foreign Policy*, July 12, 2019.

[87] Prashanth Parameswaran, "Strategic Security Dialogue Highlights US-Singapore Defense Relations," *The Diplomat*, April 29, 2019a.

ships visit Singapore monthly, and the Republic of Singapore Navy's Information Fusion Center plays a central role in improving maritime domain awareness in the region, providing information-sharing and collaboration capabilities to regional partners, including the United States.[88]

Enhancing Cooperation in New and Advanced Capabilities

Advanced technologies and capabilities with dual-use implications are also a feature of evolving U.S.-Singapore relations. According to Singapore's "total defence" concept, the nation-state prioritizes the development of advanced technologies for "digital defence" and has accordingly developed deep expertise across a variety of security-related technologies of interest to the United States.[89] As part of an Enhanced Defense Cooperation Agreement signed in 2015, the two sides agreed to cooperate in areas such as cybersecurity and biosecurity.[90] In June 2019, the United States and Singapore agreed to cooperative engagement in artificial intelligence capabilities, marked by an exchange between DoD's Joint Artificial Intelligence Center and Singapore's Defense Science and Technology Agency. The exchange focused on using artificial intelligence to enhance responses to regional humanitarian assistance and disaster relief (HA/DR) responses, but it also opened the door for further cooperation and interoperability in advanced defense technology applications more broadly.[91] Broadening this cooperation with a technologically advanced partner (Singapore), while recognizing both the challenges and opportunities afforded by Singapore's relationship with China, should be an area for continued scrutiny by the USAF and the broader DoD in the coming five to ten years.

Building on the Long-Standing Program of Exercises

Combined exercises are another important aspect of U.S.-Singapore defense cooperation, as illustrated by several exercises that enhance interoperability and give Singapore forces the opportunity to mitigate the geographic constraints they face on their small island home. The RSAF participates in Exercise Red Flag at Nellis Air Force Base in Nevada, the USAF's premier air-to-air combat training exercise, and in such exercises as Commando Sling, established in 1990 and the longest running exercise between the two air forces, and newer bilateral maritime exercises, such as Pacific Griffin (held in 2018 off Guam).[92] Ground forces have participated since 1981 in the bilateral Exercise Tiger Balm and in multilateral regional exercises involving

---

[88] H.R. Res. 374, 2016.

[89] Government of Singapore, Ministry of Defence, 2020.

[90] Parameswaran, 2019a.

[91] Prashanth Parameswaran, "What's in the New US-Singapore Artificial Intelligence Defense Partnership?" *The Diplomat*, July 1, 2019c.

[92] Prashanth Parameswaran, "US Air Force Exercise Kicks Off with Singapore's Participation," *The Diplomat*, August 17, 2017.

the United States, such as Exercise Cobra Gold.[93] Another ground force exercise, Lightning Strike, was first held in 1996 and rotates between Singapore and the United States. The latest iteration was held at Joint Base Lewis-McChord in Washington state and involved Singaporean and U.S. infantry battalions training in urban operations. Both battalions employed U.S. Stryker combat vehicles.[94]

The training and exercise opportunities afforded by cooperation with the United States are particularly important to land-starved Singapore. Basing and training space and resources for the RSAF are the bedrock of the larger strategic partnership and are a component of evolving relations between Singapore and other partners, such as India and Australia.

Singapore's Growing Defense Relations with China

In comparison, Singapore has a limited (although growing) defense relationship with China. Singapore views defense exchanges with China as part of its overall approach to managing its evolving relationship with Beijing. Official diplomatic relations between the two countries only began in 1990, and the defense component began in 2008 with the signing of the Agreement on Defense Exchanges and Security Cooperation (ADESC). As part of Singapore's duties as ASEAN Chair in 2018, the nation-state helped institute the first-ever China-ASEAN maritime exercise; in 2019, Singapore also participated in the PLA Navy's 70th Anniversary International Fleet Review.[95]

At the 2019 Shangri-La Dialogue, Chinese Defense Minister Wei Fenghe discussed several issues with Singapore's Defense Minister Ng Eng Hen. They reached agreement that a revised ADESC would include an increase in bilateral exercises, along with service-to-service and academic exchanges.[96] In October 2019, Singapore and China formalized that agreement, regularizing bilateral exercises, establishing mutual logistics support arrangements, and setting up ministerial-level dialogues.[97] The two sides are expected to hold Exercise Maritime Cooperation in 2020—the first iteration of this exercise since 2015.[98]

Even as Singapore is increasing defense ties with Beijing as a way to boost bilateral relations more generally, it is important to note this is also part of a broader trend across the region. China

---

[93] Prashanth Parameswaran, "Army Exercise Puts US-Singapore Defense Relations into Focus," *The Diplomat*, April 30, 2018.

[94] Government of Singapore, Ministry of Defence, "Singapore and US Armies Conclude Exercise Lightning Strike," press release, April 25, 2018.

[95] Prashanth Parameswaran, "What's in the New China-Singapore Deepening Military Ties Talk?" *The Diplomat*, May 30, 2019b.

[96] Parameswaran, 2019b.

[97] Aqil Haziq Mahmud, "Singapore, China Sign Defence Agreement to Scale Up Army, Navy Exercises, Establish Regular Dialogue," *CNA*, October 20, 2019.

[98] Parameswaran, 2019b.

has been trying to expand security ties with Southeast Asian countries, including U.S. allies and partners (such as Thailand and Singapore), in several ways, such as by signing new agreements, conducting exercises, and selling military equipment. For China, featuring these developments prominently is a way to showcase the progress it is making on this front, not only with Singapore but with other countries in Southeast Asia more generally.[99]

Singapore Is Enhancing Defense Relationships with Other Partners

An important component of Singapore's broader effort to strengthen its ties with other countries in the region—including Australia and India—is increased security cooperation. This activity strengthens Singapore's position in the web of U.S. allied and partner activity in the region and offers further training and interoperability opportunities for U.S. forces in the region. Singapore's security relations with Australia are particularly strong: Both nations joined the Five Power Defense Arrangement in 1971, along with the United Kingdom, New Zealand, and Malaysia, and the two sides elevated their relationship to a comprehensive strategic partnership in 2015. This partnership includes a program known as "Project 2025," which encompasses increased cooperation in economics, foreign affairs, defense, and people-to-people exchanges.[100] On the defense side, Singapore has conducted training in Australia since 1990 and, in 2016, reached an agreement to expand the number of Singaporean troops training annually in Australia from 6,000 to 14,000.[101] Although the expansion of military infrastructure required for this agreement has run into political opposition in Australia, broader security cooperation continues in several areas, from bilateral exercises (such as Exercise Trident) to enhanced intelligence and information-sharing.[102]

Although Singapore, as mentioned earlier, harbors some concerns about the potential for the U.S.-Australia-India-Japan Quadrilateral Dialogue to undermine the concept of ASEAN centrality in regional affairs, the Quad countries represent by far Singapore's most important security partners. Table 4.1 offers an overview of Singapore defense cooperation with the Quad countries (minus the United States), further emphasizing the extent to which Singapore is integrated into the broader regional landscape of U.S. alliances and security partnerships.

---

[99] The authors thank Prashanth Parameswaran for raising this point.

[100] Parameswaran, 2015.

[101] Jonathan Pearlman, "Ministers Discuss Next Stages of SAF's Training Deal," *Straits Times*, March 30, 2019.

[102] Government of Singapore, Ministry of Foreign Affairs, 2016.

Table 4.1. Singapore's Defense Cooperation with Quad Countries (Minus United States)

	Australia	Japan	India
Partnership type	Comprehensive Strategic Partnership (2015)	N/A	Strategic Partnership (2015)
2 + 2 dialogue	Yes (1996) (Joint Ministerial Committee includes trade ministers as well)	N/A	N/A
Arms sales and transfers (since 2000)	Yes (81 million trend-indicator values)[a]	N/A	N/A
Key items	N/A	N/A	N/A
Acquisition and cross-servicing agreements	N/A	N/A	N/A (a naval logistics agreement is in place as of 2018)
Defense coproduction and codevelopment	Yes	N/A	N/A
Key items	N/A	N/A	N/A
Training and military exercises	Yes	Yes	Yes
Major bilateral exercises	Ground: Matilda Air: N/A Sea: Singaroo Joint: Wallaby/Trident	No major bilateral interactions	Ground: Bold Kurukshetra Air: Joint training at Kalaikunda Air Force Station Sea: SIMBEX
Major multilateral exercises	Ground: Force 18, Bersama Lima, Bersama Shield Air: Bersama Lima, Bersama Shield, Pitch Black Sea: Bersama Lima, Bersama Shield, Kakadu, Komodo	Ground: Force 18 Air: Pitch Black, Red Flag Sea: RIMPAC, Kakadu, Komodo Joint: Cobra Gold	Ground: Force 18 Air: Pitch Black, Red Flag Sea: MILAN, RIMPAC, Kakadu, Komodo
Information-sharing agreements	Agreement for the Reciprocal Protection of Classified Information (1996)	N/A	N/A

SOURCES: Australian Government, Department of Foreign Affairs and Trade, "Singapore Country Brief," webpage, undated c; Government of Singapore, Prime Minister's Office, "Joint Statement by the Republic of Singapore and the Republic of India," Singapore, June 1, 2018; "3 Singapore Ministers to Meet Aussie Counterparts in Sydney," *Straits Times*, March 28, 2019; Government of Singapore, Ministry of Defence, "Singapore and Australia Deepen Defence Science and Technology Cooperation," press release, July 23, 2015; Government of Australia and Government of the Republic of Singapore, "Agreement Between the Government of Australia and the Government of the Republic of Singapore for the Reciprocal Protection of Classified Information Transmitted Between the Australian Department of Defence and the Singapore Ministry of Defence," Canberra, October 15, 1996; Stockholm International Peace Research Institute, "SIPRI Arms Transfers Database," webpage, undated a.

[a] The *trend-indicator value* is a unit of measurement developed by the Stockholm International Peace Research Institute. For more information, see Stockholm International Peace Research Institute, "SIPRI Arms Transfers Database – Methodology," webpage, undated b.

5. Outlook and Options

In the context of U.S. relationship-building efforts among nonalliance partners in the Indo-Pacific, strengthening relations with Singapore should be a top priority for Washington. This is particularly true in the security realm, where Singapore offers unmatched operational and logistical access for U.S. air and maritime forces adjacent to one of the world's most important shipping lanes and security chokepoints.[103] No other nation in South or Southeast Asia can, for the foreseeable future, rival Singapore as a security partner offering this geographic advantage and advanced support infrastructure.

On the diplomatic front, Singapore's position in terms of U.S. regional priorities might not rise to the same level as in the security realm, but sustaining healthy and close diplomatic ties is nonetheless important.[104] The fact that the U.S. ambassador post in Singapore has been vacant since January 2017 did not hinder recent renewal of the U.S.-Singapore security agreement granting U.S. forces access to Singapore bases, but interviews indicate that, over time, such diplomatic disconnects might hamper broader efforts by the United States to keep track of and, if necessary, counter Chinese influence operations in Southeast Asia.[105] Singapore's major role in ASEAN and its position as a target for Chinese influence operations combine to make Singapore an important nexus of U.S. regional diplomacy.

Economically, current levels of U.S. investment in and trade with Singapore provide a healthy foundation for good relations. Therefore, Singapore does not figure as prominently as some other regional actors in terms of priority for increased U.S. regional economic investment.[106] U.S.-Singapore economic interests and interactions come into play primarily in the context of regional economic dialogue and agreements. Singapore, as a key player in both the CPTPP and RCEP, can be a crucial partner in shaping the future Indo-Pacific economic environment in a way that protects U.S. interests in the face of increasing Chinese clout.

Singapore's goal to maintain a stable, rules-based regional trade and investment environment, combined with its concerns over growing Chinese influence operations in

---

[103] Dewey Sim, "Singapore Gets Fighter Jet Unit on Guam as US, Facing China Threat, Lauds Closer Ties with Allies," *South China Morning Post*, December 9, 2019b.

[104] The other reports in this series provide insight into and recommendations for U.S. diplomatic priorities in the Indo-Pacific, particularly for relationship-building efforts among nonalliance partners, such as India, Vietnam, and Indonesia.

[105] Dewey Sim, "Singapore Renews Military Bases Pact with US Amid Deepening Defence Ties with China," *South China Morning Post*, September 24, 2019a; interviews with both Singaporean and third-country, Singapore-based public policy experts, Singapore, April 2019.

[106] See the other reports in this series for analyses of where increased U.S. economic focus might best counter growing Chinese influence, particularly in areas for which BRI activity presents competitive challenges.

Singapore, point to a likely path of strategic alignment between the United States and Singapore over the course of the next decade. U.S. policymakers, however, should not underestimate the potential for a variety of more tactical developments between China and Singapore to complicate and even undermine long-term U.S.-Singapore relations and the competitive advantages the relationship provides. Incremental improvement in PRC-Singapore defense ties alone might not prove debilitating for U.S. regional posture, but such a development combined with Singaporean efforts to strengthen financial connectivity with Beijing could indicate shifts over time in Singapore's willingness to support broader U.S. regional objectives. The following sections present our assessment of the key factors involved in this strategic alignment calculus, looking ahead five to ten years in the areas of regional position and partnerships; diplomatic, economic, and defense relations; and domestic factors.

Outlook for Regional Position and Partnerships Appears to Be Increasingly Complex

In this section, we provide an assessment of the outlook for Singapore's regional position and partnerships over the next five to ten years. During this period, Singapore expects to face a more turbulent regional environment as a result of growing friction between the United States and China. As Prime Minister Lee Hsien Loong stated in August 2019, "We are all worried about the growing tensions between the United States and China. Their disputes have placed other countries in a dilemma. No country wants to take sides, and Singapore is no exception."[107]

Against this more complex backdrop of great-power competition, Singapore has reiterated its desire to promote close ties with as many regional partners as possible. It advocates a "consistent, honest, and reliable" position as an "honest broker" that can be relied on even if it means drawing the ire of either the United States or China in any given instance.[108] Principles of transparency and predictability are the bedrock of Singapore's regional outlook and engagement, according to interviews with Singaporean experts and officials.[109] However, U.S.-China tensions will affect Singapore's outlook for diplomatic, economic, and defense relations, and Singapore must be prepared to deal with new and increasingly complex realities in each of these areas.

Outlook for Diplomatic Relations Appears Challenging

Over the next five to ten years, U.S.-China competition will challenge Singapore's ability to simultaneously maintain a strong U.S. partnership and a constructive relationship with China, though it is a challenge that many believe Singapore can manage successfully, at least for now.

---

[107] Lee Hsien Loong, "Commentary: The Impact of Growing US-China Tensions on Singapore," *CNA*, August 19, 2019b.

[108] Interviews with a Singaporean government official, Singapore, April 2019.

[109] Interviews with Singaporean officials and Singapore-based foreign policy experts, Singapore, April 2019.

According to retired diplomat Bilahari Kausikan, for Singapore, "there may be no sweet spot we can occupy that will keep both the Chinese and the Americans simultaneously happy." Given this reality, Singapore seeks to pursue its interests in regional balance and, despite the difficulties, demonstrate that it won't be easily intimidated—by either Beijing or Washington.[110]

Looking ahead, Singapore can be expected to continue trying to strengthen its security partnership with the United States and to enhance its relationships with other partners to try to bolster the rules-based order in the Indo-Pacific region. However, Singapore can also be expected to try to continue to maintain a stable relationship with China, given its importance to Singapore's economy and its growing power and influence in the region and beyond. Consequently, Singapore will likely be reluctant to take actions that risk seriously undermining its relationship with China. This balancing act has worked reasonably well for Singapore so far, but it could become increasingly difficult to maintain if U.S.-China competition continues to heat up over the next five to ten years.

Outlook for Economic Relations Reflects Uncertainty—and China's Growing Clout

Singapore faces uncertainty and turbulence stemming from sharper economic competition between the United States and China generally and from the trade war since 2017 in particular. Analysts and officials in Singapore are concerned about adverse effects on the global economy. They are wary of the possibility that supply chain disruptions and restrictions on investment and research and development in China could have negative implications for Singapore's economic outlook going forward. According to Prime Minister Lee,

> Singapore is a small open economy that has benefited greatly from globalization. If U.S.-China relations continue to worsen, the world will continue to bifurcate. This augurs a more troubled future for us. Our growth will be affected. Singapore companies that export to China, and those that export to the U.S. from factories in China, will be hit.[111]

In this increasingly turbulent environment, Singapore must also consider how to contend with China's growing economic influence. Even as Singapore's economic relationship with China has grown, it is important to note that its economic ties to the United States remain very strong. As Prime Minister Lee has pointed out,

> The size and scale of U.S. investments in Singapore far out-strip any other country's. These investments create many quality jobs for Singaporeans. We also

---

[110] See Bilahari Kausikan, "No Sweet Spot for Singapore in US-China Tensions," *Straits Times*, May 30, 2019. According to Kausikan,

> Both the Chinese and Americans may not be too happy with us for pursuing our own interests. But Singapore does not exist to give joy to American or Chinese hearts. So long as neither side is so unhappy that it dismisses us as unredeemable, we can live with their unhappiness and manage it.

[111] Lee, 2019b.

> have many collaborative endeavors with US institutions, companies and experts, in the fields of innovation, research, and development.[112]

But China's economic clout is growing, and its increasingly predominant regional position and advances in the BRI and RCEP could prove challenging for the U.S. economic position over the next five to ten years. The situation could shift to a more advantageous posture, however, if the United States decides to join the CPTPP in the future.

Outlook for Defense Relations Appears to Be Very Strong Overall

Over the next five to ten years, the importance of the U.S. security partnership to Singapore is difficult to overstate. The United States will almost certainly remain Singapore's key security partner, and Singapore can be expected to purchase advanced military equipment, train with the United States and its allies and partners, provide access for U.S. forces, and work closely with the United States in counterterrorism cooperation and other areas. Singapore's defense engagement with China, by contrast, is very limited. This, however, will change in the coming decade as Singapore seeks to maintain a balance that allows it to enjoy strong relationships with the United States and China even as the two major powers are increasingly at odds.

Outlook for Domestic Factors Reflect Growing Chinese Interference and Potential Erosion of U.S. Position

Domestic factors are likely to complicate the foreign and security policy outlook for Singapore over the next five to ten years. Indeed, analysts and officials in Singapore expect the intensification of U.S.-China competition to present serious challenges in the years ahead, not only because of the cross-cutting diplomatic and economic pressures Singapore could face as a result but also, in part, because Singapore is a majority ethnic Chinese origin state. This status could lead to even more-intense pressure from Beijing to take its side in disputes with Washington as U.S.-China competition intensifies. Beijing already seeks to use this pressure as a source of leverage in its diplomatic engagement with Singapore. According to Prime Minister Lee, "Sometimes, when Singapore and China take different positions on some issue or other, our PRC friends ask us: Since we share a common heritage, a common ancestry and a common language, why does Singapore not share our common view?"[113] Kausikan has suggested that China is likely to become increasingly insistent in this regard as it seeks to pull Singapore in its direction amid growing U.S.-China competition for influence in the region.[114]

---

[112] Lee, 2019b.

[113] Lee, 2019b.

[114] See Kausikan, 2019. According to Kausikan, pressure from China is often framed in these terms: "Despite our constant denials, they still consider Singapore a 'Chinese country' and may feel entitled to our support and will not quickly forget if we are regarded as insufficiently helpful in their time of need."

At the same time, comments by some U.S. officials suggesting that U.S.-China competition could be framed as a "clash of civilizations" have heightened Singaporean concerns that Singapore's unusual status could lead to growing pressure from the United States as well as China.[115] According to Kausikan, "Some in the Trump administration also seem inclined to view the issue in racial terms. As the only ethnic Chinese-origin majority sovereign state outside greater China, we may be subject to special scrutiny."[116]

Other domestic political factors could come into play as well. Of particular note, Singapore is undergoing a transition to a new generation of leaders, a significant historical development that could influence Singapore's ability to insulate its foreign policy from domestic politics. The potential for a somewhat greater amount of domestic political contestation in Singapore, compared with previous periods during which the ruling People's Action Party has dominated politics, could complicate Singapore's efforts to maintain continuity in areas such as external relationships and defense policy.[117]

Options for the United States, the U.S. Department of Defense, and the U.S. Air Force

At a time of growing U.S.-China competition, the U.S.- Singapore partnership plays a valuable role in U.S. defense strategy in the Indo-Pacific region. Singapore's desire to maintain strong defense ties with the United States and its stepped-up engagement with other U.S. allies and partners in the region create opportunities for the United States and, specifically, for DoD and the USAF to work with Singapore and with regional partners in new and innovative ways, especially in terms of advanced technology and concepts partnerships, continued arms sales, and integrated efforts to counter malign Chinese narratives and influence operations. We present the following options for the United States, DoD, and the USAF to consider in order to take advantage of these opportunities.

Options for the United States

The U.S. government should consider the following options with respect to strengthening defense and security cooperation with Singapore in the Indo-Pacific region:

- *Continue to encourage Singapore's growing cooperation and engagement with U.S. allies, especially Australia and Japan, and emerging partners, such as India and such ASEAN states as Vietnam and Indonesia.* The United States could encourage Singapore

[115] Danson Cheong, "Xi Rejects View of China-US Row as 'Clash of Civilisations,'" *Straits Times*, May 16, 2019.

[116] Cheong, 2019.

[117] For example, topics such as Singapore's approach to defense spending and its acquisition of fighter jets were mentioned by opposition figures during Singapore's last election to a degree not seen before. The authors thank Prashanth Parameswaran for raising these points.

to continue expanding and deepening its regional relationships. The United States and Singapore should explore opportunities with Australia to develop shared objectives and priorities, particularly in the area of joint infrastructure and basing projects. Steps should be taken to expand awareness of each other's engagement activities in the region and, where possible and appropriate, coordinate their regional outreach and cooperation initiatives, particularly with respect to emerging partners. Doing so would help to ensure they will be able to focus on key objectives and maximize the effectiveness of this growing web of activities.

- *Deliberately seek opportunities to work with Singapore to counter Chinese political interference and influence operations.* Expanding cooperation in this area could consist of enhanced information-sharing and increased intelligence, cybersecurity, and law enforcement exchanges with other partners in the region and more globally. In addition, working more closely with government agencies with relevant intelligence, cybersecurity, and law enforcement responsibilities in Singapore to help them counter Chinese espionage and influence operations is an important area for greater cooperation.
- *Work privately with Singapore to counter China's narrative regarding behavior in the SCS and elsewhere.* Interviewees in Singapore uniformly recommended that the United States focus on fighting the Chinese narrative that the United States is an outsider in the SCS and is causing instability. A major component of this effort lies in reinforcing U.S. commitment to ASEAN. Other efforts should involve shining light on areas in which the Chinese are seeking opportunities to interfere with political and academic choices and freedoms and considering concrete actions to mitigate regional problems created by some BRI projects. Singapore's advice and behind-the-scenes assistance in these areas could be invaluable.

Options for the U.S. Department of Defense and the U.S. Air Force

DoD and the USAF should consider the following options to deepen their relationship with the Singaporean government:

- *Strengthen U.S.-Singapore cooperation on research and development of advanced capabilities and further enhance U.S.-Singapore cooperation in the areas of advanced cyber, artificial intelligence, and command, control, communications, computers, intelligence, surveillance, and reconnaissance.* Building on the initial efforts we described earlier, the United States can further enhance cooperation with Singapore in areas including information-sharing and artificial intelligence applications. The two countries could focus on increasing collaboration in the science and technology communities, where there exists a shared culture of experimentation and innovation. The United States and Singapore should also consider emphasizing areas in which cooperation could contribute to the development of new capabilities, especially ones that could strengthen deterrence of China by complicating Chinese planning and decisionmaking: areas such as maritime surveillance and reconnaissance, underwater detection, and advanced cybersecurity.
- *Incrementally increase the current trajectory of both security assistance and operational interface (training, exercises, arms sales).* Assurance of continued or increased U.S. prioritization of the relationship, and the value of the region in general to the U.S. Indo-Pacific strategy, is the cornerstone of U.S. advantage in the competition with China.

Maintaining operational and logistical access and support at the juncture of the Straits of Malacca and the Indian Ocean and leveraging Singapore's influence in ASEAN and deep connectivity in the web of U.S. regional alliances and partnerships make the investment of time and treasure with Singapore a key component of U.S Indo-Pacific strategy. The U.S. sale of F-35s is a major success story, and Singapore might want additional sales moving forward.

- *Consider extending special dispensation to facilitate arms sales to other countries in the region.* Some Singapore discussants also recommended that the United States consider extending special dispensation (and prices) to other actors in the region in terms of arms sales: Although Singapore can afford U.S. arms, many potential partners in the region cannot and therefore turn to other sources to fill needs.
- *Work with Singapore on HA/DR and other traditional and nontraditional security activities*. DoD and the USAF should consider taking advantage of opportunities to collaborate more closely in infrastructure, security, and surveillance; institutional capacity-building; and HA/DR. In terms of infrastructure, access is a key component to U.S. strategy in the region, and improving infrastructure at key facilities will likely improve access for all. There are several key areas where the United States can work directly with Singapore to build capacity there and can work with Singapore to build capacity for other partners in Southeast Asia. These areas include maritime domain awareness, counterpiracy, and counterterrorism, and activities can encompass expanded training space and improved facilities and increased operational interface and exercises. These activities can deliver a great deal of goodwill regionally and mitigate some of the challenges the United States and Singapore face if all their cooperative efforts appear focused on military balancing against China.[118]

[118] Interviews with Singapore-based regional security and China policy experts, Singapore, April 2019.

Appendix. Detailed Framework Variable Coding

This report is part of a series of country studies that assess the competition for influence in these nations between China and the United States. The main report, *Regional Responses to U.S.-China Competition in the Indo-Pacific: Study Overview and Conclusions*, presents a detailed explanation of a RAND-developed analytic framework for evaluating which competitor, China or the United States, maintains the most influence in a given third country.[119] To offer readers of this report additional details on the framework, Table A.1 briefly explains the color coding of the RAND framework variables. The rest of the appendix presents the sources that supported the framework's variables.

Table A.1. Color Coding of Framework Variables

Variable	Coding
Diplomatic and political	
Diplomatic and political ties	• **Blue:** Partner has significantly closer diplomatic ties with the United States than China and prioritizes its relationship with the United States. • **Light blue:** Partner has slightly closer diplomatic ties with the United States than China and places relatively more priority on ties with the United States. • **Gray:** Partner has similar diplomatic ties with the United States and China and attaches similar weight to relations with the United States and China. • **Light red:** Partner has slightly closer diplomatic ties with China than the United States and places relatively more priority on ties with China. • **Red:** Partner has significantly closer diplomatic ties with China than the United States and prioritizes its relationship with China.
Support for U.S. versus Chinese vision for the region	• **Blue:** Partner views the U.S. vision for the region as highly aligned with its own interests and is concerned that China's vision undermines its interests. • **Light blue:** Partner views the U.S. vision for the region as generally more aligned with its own interests than China's visions. • **Gray:** Partner views both visions as similarly aligned with its interests, *or* the partner views neither vision as aligned with its interests. • **Light red:** Partner views the Chinese vision for the region as generally more aligned with its own interests than the U.S. vision. • **Red:** Partner views the Chinese vision for the region as highly aligned with its own interests and is concerned that the U.S. vision undermines its interests.
Views of U.S. commitment to the region	• **Blue:** Partner is very confident that the United States will remain committed to the region and will at least maintain its current level of attention to the region, and partner can rely on the United States. • **Light blue:** Partner is cautiously optimistic that the United States will remain committed to the region and will likely maintain its current level of attention to the region; and partner can rely on the United States.

[119] Bonny Lin, Michael S. Chase, Jonah Blank, Cortez A. Cooper III, Derek Grossman, Scott W. Harold, Jennifer D. P. Maroney, Lyle J. Morris, Logan Ma, Paul Orner, Alice Shih, and Soo Kim, *Regional Responses to U.S.-China Competition in the Indo-Pacific: Study Overview and Conclusions*, Santa Monica, Calif.: RAND Corporation, RR-4412-AF, 2020.

Variable	Coding
	• **Gray:** Partner is uncertain whether the United States will remain committed to the region, is uncertain that the United States will maintain its current level of attention to the region, and is uncertain that it can rely on the United States. • **Light red:** Partner is relatively pessimistic that the United States will remain committed to the region, believes that the United States will have difficulty maintaining attention toward the region, and does not believe that it can rely on the United States. • **Red:** Partner does not believe that the United States is committed to the region, believes that the United States is likely to decrease its attention to the region, and does not believe that it can rely on the United States.
Public opinion	• **Blue:** Partner public opinion significantly favors the United States over China by more than 20 percent. • **Light blue:** Partner public opinion slightly favors the United States over China by 3 percent to 20 percent. • **Gray:** Partner public opinion has similar favorability views of the United States and China. • **Light red:** Partner public opinion slightly favors China over the United States by 3 percent to 20 percent. • **Red:** Partner public opinion significantly favors China over the United States by more than 20 percent.
Economic	
Economic dependence	• **Blue:** Partner is significantly dependent on trade, investment, and (to a lesser extent) tourism from the United States, compared with China (more than 20 percent). • **Light blue:** Partner is moderately more dependent on trade, investment, and (to a lesser extent) tourism from the United States, compared with China (3 percent to 20 percent). • **Gray:** Partner is similarly dependent on trade, investment, and (to a lesser extent) tourism from the United States, compared with China. • **Light red:** Partner is moderately more dependent on trade, investment, and (to a lesser extent) tourism from China, compared to the United States (3 percent to 20 percent). • **Red:** Partner is significantly dependent on trade, investment, and (to a lesser extent) tourism from China, compared with the United States (more than 20 percent).
Economic opportunity	• **Blue:** Partner strongly believes that it will depend more on trade and investments with the United States than China in the next 10–15 years. • **Light blue:** Partner believes that it is likely to depend more on trade and investments with the United States than China in the next 10–15 years. • **Gray:** Partner believes that it is likely to depend as much on the United States as on China for trade and investment in the next 10–15 years. • **Light red:** Partner believes that it is likely to depend more on trade and investments with China than the United States in the next 10–15 years. • **Red:** Partner strongly believes that it will depend more on trade and investments with China than the United States in the next 10–15 years.
Threat perceptions of the United States versus China (economic)	• **Blue:** Partner has significant concerns regarding U.S. economic influence and views U.S. economic strength as threatening, subversive, or coercive. • **Light blue:** Partner has some, but limited, concerns regarding U.S. economic influence and views U.S. economic strength as threatening, subversive, or coercive. • **Gray:** Partner does not view the United States and China as economic threats *or* has equal concerns about negative U.S. and Chinese economic influence. • **Light red:** Partner has some, but limited, concerns regarding Chinese economic influence and views Chinese economic strength as threatening, subversive, or coercive.

Variable	Coding
	• **Red:** Partner has significant concerns regarding Chinese economic influence and views Chinese economic strength as threatening, subversive, or coercive.
Willingness to work with the United States versus China based on economic threat perceptions	• **Blue:** Partner seeks to work with the United States to counter or mitigate assessed Chinese economic threats and has taken significant measures to reduce economic dependency on China. • **Light blue:** Partner seeks greater economic cooperation with the United States and has taken some measures to limit or reduce Chinese economic influence in key economic sectors. • **Gray:** Partner seeks greater economic cooperation with the United States and China and seeks economic diversification to avoid overdependence on either country. • **Light red:** Partner seeks greater economic cooperation with China and has taken some measures to limit or reduce U.S. economic influence in key economic sectors. • **Red:** Partner seeks to work with China to counter or balance against assessed U.S. economic threat and has taken significant measures to reduce economic dependency on the United States.
Military and security	
Threat perceptions of the United States versus China (military)	• **Blue:** Partner views the United States as a significant military or security threat. • **Light blue:** Partner views the United States as a limited military or security threat. • **Gray:** Partner does not view the United States and China as military or security threats *or* has equal concerns about both countries. • **Light red:** Partner views China as a limited military or security threat. • **Red:** Partner views China as a significant military or security threat.
Willingness to work with the United States versus China based on military threat perceptions	• **Blue:** Partner seeks increased cooperation with the United States to balance against assessed Chinese military or security threat and has taken actions to directly or indirectly balance against China's military strength. • **Light blue:** Partner seeks increased cooperation with the United States to strengthen its own military capabilities, has taken some measures to address perceived Chinese military threat, and is cautious of directly balancing against China. • **Gray:** Partner seeks more military cooperation with the United States and China *or* partner's willingness to militarily cooperate with the United States or China is not driven by U.S. or China military threat perceptions. • **Light red:** Partner seeks increased cooperation with China to strengthen its own military capabilities; has taken some measures to address perceived U.S. military threat and is cautious of directly balancing against the United States. • **Red:** Partner seeks increased cooperation with China to balance against assessed U.S. military or security threat and has taken actions to directly or indirectly balance against U.S. military strength.
Support for major U.S.-led security efforts	• **Blue:** Partner has participated or supported many key U.S.-led international and regional security efforts. • **Light blue:** Partner has participated or supported some U.S.-led international and regional security efforts. • **Gray:** Partner has shown limited or no support to U.S.-led international and regional security efforts. • **Light red:** Partner has opposed some U.S.-led international and regional security efforts. • **Red:** Partner has opposed many U.S.-led international or regional security efforts.
Military cooperation	• **Blue:** Partner has significantly closer military ties with the United States than China and engages in significantly more military activities and cooperation with the United States.

Variable	Coding
	• **Light blue:** Partner has slightly closer military ties with the United States than China and engages in moderately more military activities and cooperation with the United States. • **Gray:** Partner has similar military ties with the United States and China and attaches similar weight to defense and security cooperation with the United States and China. • **Light red:** Partner has slightly closer military ties with China than the United States and engages in moderately more military activities and cooperation with China. • **Red:** Partner has significantly closer military ties with China than the United States and engages in significantly more military activities and cooperation with China.
U.S. versus Chinese military capability	• **Blue:** Partner believes that the United States currently has a significant military advantage over China in terms of military capabilities. • **Light blue:** Partner believes that the United States currently has a modest military advantage over China in terms of military capabilities. • **Gray:** Partner believes that the United States and China have similar military capabilities. • **Light red:** Partner believes that China currently has a modest military advantage over the United States in terms of military capabilities. • **Red:** Partner believes that China currently has a significant military advantage over the United States in terms of military capabilities.
Perception of U.S. willingness to aid partner in conflict with China	• **Blue:** Partner is confident that the United States will provide military support or aid if partner becomes involved in a potential military conflict with China. • **Light blue:** Partner is cautiously optimistic that the United States will provide military support or aid if partner becomes involved in a potential military conflict with China. • **Gray:** Partner is uncertain whether the United States will provide military support or aid if partner becomes involved in a potential military conflict with China. • **Light red:** Partner is pessimistic that the United States will provide military support or aid if partner becomes involved in a potential military conflict with China. • **Red:** Partner does not believe that the United States will provide military support or aid if partner becomes involved in a potential military conflict with China.

NOTE: Variables measuring shared interests are roman, and variables measuring relative capability are italicized.

Variable: Diplomatic and Political Ties

- **Coding method:** Researchers coded based on interviews and analysis.
- **Data sources in addition to interviews:** U.S. Department of State, "Websites of U.S. Embassies, Consulates, and Diplomatic Missions," webpage, undated c; U.S. Department of State, homepage, undated a; U.S. Department of State, "Press Releases," webpage, undated b; Stockholm International Peace Research Institute, "SIPRI Arms Transfers Database," webpage, undated a; White House, "Briefings & Statements," webpage, undated b; White House, "Barack Obama," webpage, undated a; White House, "George W. Bush," webpage, undated c.
- **Notes:** We do not use UN voting as an indicator of diplomatic interests. U.S. interests go beyond issues voted on at the UN. Countries vote on a variety of issues in the UN that are not of equal strategic importance to the United States. Among the subset of UN votes that the U.S. Department of State categorizes as important for the United States, a good

proportion relates to Israel and Palestine, and the majority of the issues relate to general development or foreign policy concerns that are not specific to security issues in the Indo-Pacific. In 2017, for example, among the State Department–identified important UN votes, there was only one vote—situation of human rights in Burma—out of 27 votes that was specific to the Indo-Pacific. [120]

Variable: Support for U.S. Versus Chinese Vision for the Region

- **Coding method:** Researchers coded based on interviews and data from various polling sources.
- **Data source in addition to interviews:** Tang Siew Mun, Moe Thuzar, Hoang Thi Ha, Termsak Chalermpalanupap, Pham Thi Phuong Thao, and Anuthida Saelaow Qian, *The State of Southeast Asia: 2019 Survey Report*, Singapore: ISEAS–Yusof Ishak Institute, 2019.

Variable: Views of U.S. Commitment to the Region

- **Coding method:** Researchers coded based on interviews and data from various polling sources.
- **Data sources in addition to interviews:** Japanese Ministry of Foreign Affairs, "Opinion Poll on Japan in ASEAN Countries," March 2019; Tang Siew Mun, Moe Thuzar, Hoang Thi Ha, Termsak Chalermpalanupap, Pham Thi Phuong Thao, and Anuthida Saelaow Qian, *The State of Southeast Asia: 2019 Survey Report*, Singapore: ISEAS–Yusof Ishak Institute, 2019.

Variable: Public Opinion

- **Coding method:** Researchers coded based on interviews and polling data on whether the country has favorable views of the United States or China. The calculations used U.S. favorability (percentage) minus PRC favorability (percentage).
- **Data sources in addition to interviews:** Pew Research Center, Global Indicators Database, "Australia: Opinion of the United States," updated August 2017; Tang Siew Mun, Moe Thuzar, Hoang Thi Ha, Termsak Chalermpalanupap, Pham Thi Phuong Thao, and Anuthida Saelaow Qian, *The State of Southeast Asia: 2019 Survey Report*, Singapore: ISEAS–Yusof Ishak Institute, 2019; Yun-han Chu, Yu-tzung Chang, and Min-hua Huang, "How East Asians View the Influence of United States vs. a Rising China," Hu Fu Center for East Asia Democratic Studies, National Taiwan University, 2016; Wan Saiful Wan Jan, "Malaysians' Response to Big China Presence Shows Concerns," *Straits Times*, April 27, 2017; Boo Su-Lyn, "Malaysians More Positive About China Now, Studies Show," *Malay Mail*, April 1, 2017; Johannes Herlijanto, *Public Perceptions of China in Indonesia: The Indonesia National Survey*, Singapore: ISEAS–Yusof Ishak Institute, December 4, 2017a; Bruce Stokes, Dorothy Manevich, and Hanyu

---

[120] U.S. Department of State, *Voting Practices in the United Nations 2017*, Washington, D.C., March 2018; Sarah Rose, *Linking US Foreign Aid to UN Votes: What Are the Implications?* Washington, D.C.: Center for Global Development, May 2018.

Chwe, "India and the World," Pew Research Center, November 15, 2017; Johannes Herlijanto, "Public Perceptions of China in Indonesia: The Indonesia National Survey," *Belt and Road*, December 5, 2017b; Globe Scan, "Sharp Drop in World Views of US, UK: Global Poll," July 4, 2017.

Variable: Economic Dependence

- **Coding method:** Researchers coded based on 65 percent trade (the difference in the country's trade with the United States versus China), 20 percent inward FDI (the difference in the United States versus PRC FDI into the country), 10 percent outward FDI (the difference in the country's FDI in the United States versus the country's FDI in China), and 5 percent tourism (the difference in U.S. tourism to the country versus Chinese tourism to the country). Five percent is reflective of the economic importance of tourism to regional countries.[121]
- **Data sources in addition to interviews:** Researchers used the most recent year data available (2017 or 2018) and partner reporting for trade. Researchers used U.S. sources for U.S. FDI and partner FDI in the United States and Chinese sources for Chinese FDI and partner FDI in China. United Nations, "UN Comtrade Database," webpage, undated; United Nations Conference on Trade and Development, *World Investment Report 2018: Investment and New Industrial Policies*, Geneva, Switzerland: United Nations Publications, 2018; U.S. Bureau of Economic Analysis, "Direct Investment by Country and Industry," webpage, updated July 24, 2019; U.S. Bureau of Economic Analysis, "Foreign Direct Investment in the U.S.: Balance of Payments and Direct Investment Position Data," webpage, updated June 19, 2020; Chinese Ministry of Commerce, *2017 Statistical Bulletin of China's Outward Foreign Direct Investment,* Beijing, October 2018.
- **Notes:** We also examined trade imbalance, including dependency on particular import or export products. As indicated in the main text, we also explored placing more weight on partner exports as compared with imports.

Variable: Economic Opportunity

- **Coding method:** Researchers coded based on interviews and projected U.S. and Chinese economic growth rates.
- **Data sources in addition to interviews:** U.S. Bureau of Economic Analysis, "Direct Investment by Country and Industry," webpage, updated July 24, 2019; U.S. Bureau of Economic Analysis, "Foreign Direct Investment in the U.S.: Balance of Payments and Direct Investment Position Data," webpage, updated June 19, 2020; American Enterprise Institute and Heritage Foundation, China Global Investment Tracker, homepage, undated; International Monetary Fund, "World Economic Outlook Database October 2018," October 9, 2018; Transparency International, "Corruption Perceptions Index: 2018," webpage, 2018; Chinese Ministry of Commerce; PricewaterhouseCoopers, *The Long View: How Will the Global Economic Order Change by 2050?* London, February 2017;

[121] Yuwa Hedrick-Wong, "Asia's Economic Ties Strengthen Amid Gathering Global Storm," *Forbes*, September 30, 2018.

Lowy Institute, *Asia Power Index 2019*, Sydney, 2019; "The World's Economic Powerhouses Are Going to Look Very Different in Another Decade," *News.com.au*, January 20, 2019; Will Martin, "The U.S. Could Lose Its Crown as the World's Most Powerful Economy as Soon as Next Year, and It's Unlikely to Ever Get It Back," *Business Insider*, January 10, 2019; Janet Henry and James Pomeroy, *The World in 2030*, London: HSBC, September 2019.

Variable: Threat Perceptions of the United States Versus China (Economic)

- **Coding method:** Researchers coded based on interviews, literature review, and polling data.
- **Data sources in addition to interviews:** Tang Siew Mun, Moe Thuzar, Hoang Thi Ha, Termsak Chalermpalanupap, Pham Thi Phuong Thao, and Anuthida Saelaow Qian, *The State of Southeast Asia: 2019 Survey Report*, Singapore: ISEAS–Yusof Ishak Institute, 2019; Natasha Kassam, *Lowy Institute Poll 2019*, Sydney: Lowy Institute, June 2019.

Variable: Willingness to Work with the United States Versus China Based on Economic Threat Perceptions

- **Coding method:** Researchers coded based on interviews and literature review.
- **Data sources in addition to interviews:** Tang Siew Mun, Moe Thuzar, Hoang Thi Ha, Termsak Chalermpalanupap, Pham Thi Phuong Thao, and Anuthida Saelaow Qian, *The State of Southeast Asia: 2019 Survey Report*, Singapore: ISEAS–Yusof Ishak Institute, 2019; Natasha Kassam, *Lowy Institute Poll 2019*, Sydney: Lowy Institute, June 2019.

Variable: Threat Perceptions of the United States Versus China (Military)

- **Coding method:** Researchers coded based on interviews, literature review, and polling data.
- **Data sources in addition to interviews:** Tang Siew Mun, Moe Thuzar, Hoang Thi Ha, Termsak Chalermpalanupap, Pham Thi Phuong Thao, and Anuthida Saelaow Qian, *The State of Southeast Asia: 2019 Survey Report*, Singapore: ISEAS–Yusof Ishak Institute, 2019; Natasha Kassam, *Lowy Institute Poll 2019*, Sydney: Lowy Institute, June 2019.

Variable: Willingness to Work with the United States Versus China Based on Military Threat Perceptions

- **Coding method:** Researchers coded based on interviews and literature review.
- **Data sources in addition to interviews:** Tang Siew Mun, Moe Thuzar, Hoang Thi Ha, Termsak Chalermpalanupap, Pham Thi Phuong Thao, and Anuthida Saelaow Qian, *The State of Southeast Asia: 2019 Survey Report*, Singapore: ISEAS–Yusof Ishak Institute, 2019; Natasha Kassam, *Lowy Institute Poll 2019*, Sydney: Lowy Institute, June 2019.

Variable: Support for Major U.S.-Led Security Efforts

- **Coding method:** Researchers coded an aggregate of data collected on how regional countries support or participate in U.S.-led international or regional initiatives: If countries supported major U.S. efforts related to North Korea, including efforts to disrupt North Korean ship-to-ship transfers; participated in SCS patrols, operations, or major exercises with the United States in SCS international waters; engaged in Taiwan Strait transits; supported U.S. freedom of navigation operations; participated in major U.S.-led military operations (Operation Enduring Freedom, International Security Assistance Force, Operation Iraqi Freedom, and Operation Inherent Resolve); and participated in the Global Coalition to Defeat ISIS.
- **Data sources in addition to interviews:** Various articles from the Council on Foreign Relations, *The Diplomat*, Reuters, *The Guardian*, BBC, *Japan Times*, the Australian Strategic Policy Institute, and foreign ministry websites.

Variable: Military Cooperation

- **Coding method:** Researchers coded as an aggregate of six measures: if the United States or China has a major military base or facility in the country; relative U.S. versus Chinese arms sales to the country; whether the country has acquisition and cross-servicing agreements with the United States versus a similar agreement with China; whether the country has defense coproduction and codevelopment agreements with the United States, compared with similar agreements with China; whether the country has an information-sharing agreement with the United States, compared with a similar agreement with China; and how much the country militarily trains and exercises with the United States, compared with China.
- **Data sources in addition to interviews:** Various articles in the *China Daily* and *People's Daily*; Kenneth W. Allen, John Chen, and Phillip Charles Saunders, *Chinese Military Diplomacy, 2003–2016: Trends and Implications*, Washington, D.C.: National Defense University Press, 2017; Defense Intelligence Agency, *China Military Power: Modernizing a Force to Fight and Win*, Washington, D.C., 2019; U.S. Department of Defense and U.S. Department of State, *Fiscal Years 2017 and 2018 Joint Report to Congress*, Vol. 1, Washington, D.C., Foreign Military Training Report F-685A5A8, November 27, 2017a; U.S. Department of Defense and U.S. Department of State, *Fiscal Years 2017 and 2018 Joint Report to Congress*, Vol. 2: *Country Training Activities*, Washington, D.C., Foreign Military Training Report F-685A5A8, November 27, 2017b; U.S. Department of Defense and U.S. Department of State, *Fiscal Years 2018 and 2019 Joint Report to Congress*, Vol. 1, Washington, D.C., Foreign Military Training Report 2-C52504A, March 13, 2019a; U.S. Department of Defense and U.S. Department of State, *Fiscal Years 2018 and 2019 Joint Report to Congress*, Vol. 2: *Country Training Activities*, Washington, D.C., Foreign Military Training Report 2-C52504A, March 13, 2019b; U.S. Department of Defense, *Annual Report to Congress: Military and Security Developments Involving the People's Republic of China 2019*, Washington, D.C.: Office of the Secretary of Defense, E-1F4B924, May 2, 2019; U.S. Department of Defense, *Assessment on U.S. Defense Implications of China's Expanding Global Access*, Washington, D.C.: Office of the Secretary of Defense, 6-6B48CD8, December 20, 2018;

Stockholm International Peace Research Institute, "SIPRI Arms Transfers Database," webpage, undated a; U.S. Army Pacific, homepage, undated; Commander, U.S. Pacific Fleet, homepage, undated; Chinese Embassy in Thailand, homepage, undated;[122] State Council of the People's Republic of China, *The Diversified Employment of China's Armed Forces*, Beijing, 2013; State Council of the People's Republic of China, *China's Military Strategy*, Beijing, 2015; State Council of the People's Republic of China, *China's Policies on Asia-Pacific Security Cooperation*, Beijing, 2017; State Council of the People's Republic of China, *China's Foreign Aid*, Beijing, 2014.

Variable: U.S. Versus Chinese Military Capability

- **Coding method:** Researchers coded based on regional interviews and comparisons of current U.S. versus PRC military capability.
- **Data sources in addition to interviews:** Lowy Institute, *Asia Power Index 2019*, Sydney, 2019; International Institute for Strategic Studies, "Asia," in *The Military Balance 2019*, London, 2019, pp. 222–319.

Variable: Perception of U.S. Willingness to Aid Country in Conflict with China

- **Coding method:** Researchers coded based on interviews, literature review, and polling data.
- **Data sources in addition to interviews:** Stafford Nichols and Zacc Ritter, "U.S. Defense Promise Still Credible in Asia-Pacific," Gallup, July 17, 2018; Tang Siew Mun, Moe Thuzar, Hoang Thi Ha, Termsak Chalermpalanupap, Pham Thi Phuong Thao, and Anuthida Saelaow Qian, *The State of Southeast Asia: 2019 Survey Report*, Singapore: ISEAS–Yusof Ishak Institute, 2019.

[122] This source is provided as an example. All of China's embassy websites that were of interest to this report were used.

References

"3 Singapore Ministers to Meet Aussie Counterparts in Sydney," *Straits Times*, March 28, 2019.

Allen, Kenneth W., John Chen, and Phillip Charles Saunders, *Chinese Military Diplomacy, 2003–2016: Trends and Implications*, Washington, D.C.: National Defense University Press, 2017.

American Enterprise Institute and Heritage Foundation, China Global Investment Tracker, homepage, undated. As of October 23, 2019: https://www.aei.org/china-global-investment-tracker/?ncid=txtlnkusaolp00000618?

Ariffin, Afifah, "ASEAN Chair: Singapore Has Accomplished Far More Than Anticipated," *CNA*, November 11, 2018.

"Asia Loses Confidence in US Leadership," *Asia Sentinel*, June 4, 2019. As of September 12, 2019: https://www.asiasentinel.com/econ-business/asia-loses-confidence-usa-leadership/

Australian Government, Department of Foreign Affairs and Trade, "ASEAN-Australia-New Zealand FTA," webpage, undated a. As of October 23, 2019: https://dfat.gov.au/trade/agreements/in-force/aanzfta/Pages/asean-australia-new-zealand-free-trade-agreement.aspx

———, "Singapore-Australia FTA," webpage, undated b. As of October 23, 2019: https://dfat.gov.au/trade/agreements/in-force/safta/Pages/singapore-australia-fta.aspx

———, "Singapore Country Brief," webpage, undated c. As of July 20, 2020: https://www.dfat.gov.au/geo/singapore/Pages/singapore-country-brief

Balakrishnan, Vivian, "MFA Press Release: Speech by Minister for Foreign Affairs Dr Vivian Balakrishnan During the Committee of Supply Debate, 1 March 2018," Singapore: Ministry of Foreign Affairs, March 1, 2018. As of July 20, 2020: https://www.mfa.gov.sg/Newsroom/Press-Statements-Transcripts-and-Photos/2018/03/Min-COS-2018-Speech

Bei Yi, Seow, "ASEAN Has to Work with the World as It Is: PM Lee Hsien Loong," *Straits Times*, November 15, 2018.

Carey, Glen, and Philip Heijmans, "Singapore Urges U.S. to Accept China as Competitor," *Bloomberg*, updated May 17, 2019. As of October 23, 2019: https://www.bloomberg.com/news/articles/2019-05-16/singapore-urges-u-s-to-accept-china-s-rise-spare-other-nations

Caverly, Jonathan D., Ethan B. Kapstein, and Srdjan Vucetic, "F-35 Sales Are America's Belt and Road," *Foreign Policy*, July 12, 2019.

Center for Strategic and International Studies, China Power Project, "Is China Both a Source and Hub for International Students?" webpage, undated. As of September 12, 2019: https://chinapower.csis.org/china-international-students/

Cheong, Danson, "Xi Rejects View of China-US Row as 'Clash of Civilisations,'" *Straits Times*, May 16, 2019.

"China Military Paying 'Close Attention' to US Plane Deployment in Singapore," *Straits Times*, December 9, 2015. As of September 12, 2019: https://www.straitstimes.com/asia/east-asia/china-military-paying-close-attention-to-us-plane-deployment-in-singapore

Chinese Embassy in Thailand, homepage, undated. As of June 25, 2020: http://www.chinaembassy.or.th/eng/

Chinese Ministry of Commerce, *2017 Statistical Bulletin of China's Outward Foreign Direct Investment,* Beijing, October 2018.

Chu, Yun-han, Yu-tzung Chang, and Min-hua Huang, "How East Asians View the Influence of United States vs. a Rising China," Hu Fu Center for East Asia Democratic Studies, National Taiwan University, 2016.

Commander, U.S. Pacific Fleet, homepage, undated. As of June 25, 2020: https://www.cpf.navy.mil

Cronin, Patrick M., "US Asia Strategy: Beyond the Quad," *The Diplomat*, March 9, 2019.

Defense Intelligence Agency, *China Military Power: Modernizing a Force to Fight and Win*, Washington, D.C., 2019.

Fook, Lye Liang, "Singapore–China Relations: Building Substantive Ties Amidst Challenges," *Southeast Asian Affairs*, 2018, pp. 321–340.

Gady, Franz-Stefan, "US Navy Littoral Combat Ship Arrives in Singapore for Rotational Deployment," *The Diplomat,* July 9, 2019.

Globe Scan, "Sharp Drop in World Views of US, UK: Global Poll," July 4, 2017.

Government of Australia and Government of the Republic of Singapore, "Agreement Between the Government of Australia and the Government of the Republic of Singapore for the Reciprocal Protection of Classified Information Transmitted Between the Australian Department of Defence and the Singapore Ministry of Defence," Canberra, October 15, 1996.

Government of India, Department of Commerce, "Indian Trade Portal," webpage, undated. As of October 23, 2019: https://www.indiantradeportal.in/vs.jsp?lang=1&id=0,1,63,68

Government of Singapore, Ministry of Defence, "Singapore and Australia Deepen Defence Science and Technology Cooperation," press release, July 23, 2015.

———, "Singapore and US Armies Conclude Exercise Lightning Strike," press release, April 25, 2018.

———, "Defence Policy and Diplomacy," webpage, updated March 4, 2019. As of July 21, 2020: https://www.mindef.gov.sg/web/portal/mindef/defence-matters/defence-topic/defence-topic-detail/defence-policy-and-diplomacy

———, "Total Defence," webpage, updated February 20, 2020. As of July 21, 2020: https://www.mindef.gov.sg/web/portal/mindef/defence-matters/defence-topic/defence-topic-detail/total-defence

Government of Singapore, Ministry of Foreign Affairs, "ASEAN," webpage, undated a. As of September 12, 2019: https://www.mfa.gov.sg/SINGAPORES-FOREIGN-POLICY/International-Organisations/ASEAN

———, "India," webpage, undated b. As of July 20, 2020: https://www.mfa.gov.sg/SINGAPORES-FOREIGN-POLICY/Countries-and-Regions/South-Asia/India

———, "Japan," webpage, undated c. As of September 12, 2019: https://www.mfa.gov.sg/SINGAPORES-FOREIGN-POLICY/Countries-and-Regions/Northeast-Asia/Japan

———, "People's Republic of China," webpage, undated d. As of September 12, 2019: https://www.mfa.gov.sg/SINGAPORES-FOREIGN-POLICY/Countries-and-Regions/Northeast-Asia/Peoples-Republic-of-China

———, "MFA Press Statement: Singapore-Australia Comprehensive Strategic Partnership Package," press release, May 6, 2016. As of September 12, 2019: https://www.mfa.gov.sg/Newsroom/Press-Statements-Transcripts-and-Photos/2016/05/MFA-Press-Statement-SingaporeAustralia-Comprehensive-Strategic-Partnership-Package-6-May-2016

Government of Singapore, Prime Minister's Office, "Joint Statement by the Republic of Singapore and the Republic of India," Singapore, June 1, 2018.

———, "PM Lee Hsien Loong at the IISS Shangri-La Dialogue 2019," May 31, 2019. As of September 12, 2019: https://www.pmo.gov.sg/Newsroom/PM-Lee-Hsien-Loong-at-the-IISS-Shangri-La-Dialogue-2019

Government of Singapore, Singapore Tourism Board, "International Visitor Arrivals," webpage, undated. As of September 12, 2019: https://www.stb.gov.sg/content/stb/en/statistics-and-market-insights/tourism-statistics/international-visitorarrivals.html

Han, Kristen, "The Guessing Game for Singapore's Elections," *The Interpreter*, July 16, 2019. As of September 12, 2019: https://www.lowyinstitute.org/the-interpreter/guessing-game-singapore-elections

Hedrick-Wong, Yuwa, "Asia's Economic Ties Strengthen Amid Gathering Global Storm," *Forbes*, September 30, 2018.

Henry, Janet, and James Pomeroy, *The World in 2030*, London: HSBC, September 2019.

Herlijanto, Johannes, *Public Perceptions of China in Indonesia: The Indonesia National Survey*, Singapore: ISEAS–Yusof Ishak Institute, December 4, 2017a.

———, "Public Perceptions of China in Indonesia: The Indonesia National Survey," *Belt and Road*, December 5, 2017b.

Hsiao, Russell, "A Preliminary Survey of CCP Influence Operations in Singapore," *China Brief*, July 16, 2019. As of September 12, 2019: https://jamestown.org/program/a-preliminary-survey-of-ccp-influence-operations-in-singapore/

Hunt, Luke, "How Close Is RCEP to Reality?" *The Diplomat*, October 16, 2019.

International Institute for Strategic Studies, "Asia," in *The Military Balance 2019*, London, 2019, pp. 222–319.

International Monetary Fund, "World Economic Outlook Database October 2018," October 9, 2018. As of July 20, 2020: https://www.imf.org/external/pubs/ft/weo/2018/02/weodata/index.aspx

Jacobs, Andrew, "In Singapore, Vitriol Against Chinese Newcomers," *New York Times*, July 26, 2012.

Jan, Wan Saiful Wan, "Malaysians' Response to Big China Presence Shows Concerns," *Straits Times*, April 27, 2017.

Japanese Ministry of Foreign Affairs, "Opinion Poll on Japan in ASEAN Countries," March 2019.

Kassam, Natasha, *Lowy Institute Poll 2019*, Sydney: Lowy Institute, June 2019. As of June 22, 2020: https://www.lowyinstitute.org/publications/lowy-institute-poll-2019

Kausikan, Bilahari, "Singapore Cannot Be Cowed by Size," *Straits Times*, July 3, 2017.

———, "No Sweet Spot for Singapore in US-China Tensions," *Straits Times*, May 30, 2019.

Lai, Linette, "Parliament: Vivian Outlines Foreign Policy Challenges Singapore Faces and How It Will Overcome Them," *Straits Times*, March 1, 2019. As of September 12, 2019: https://www.straitstimes.com/politics/parliament-vivian-outlines-foreign-policy-challenges-singapore-faces-and-how-it-will

Lee Hsien Loong, "Commentary: From Singapore to Singaporeans, the Making of a National Identity," *CNA*, August 19, 2019a.

———, "Commentary: The Impact of Growing US-China Tensions on Singapore," *CNA*, August 19, 2019b.

Lin, Bonny, Michael S. Chase, Jonah Blank, Cortez A. Cooper III, Derek Grossman, Scott W. Harold, Jennifer D. P. Maroney, Lyle J. Morris, Logan Ma, Paul Orner, Alice Shih, and Soo Kim, *Regional Responses to U.S.-China Competition in the Indo-Pacific: Study Overview and Conclusions*, Santa Monica, Calif.: RAND Corporation, RR-4412-AF, 2020.

Lowy Institute, *Asia Power Index 2019*, Sydney, 2019.

Mahbubani, Kishore, "Qatar: Big Lessons from a Small Country," *Straits Times*, July 1, 2017.

Mahmud, Aqil Haziq, "Singapore, China Sign Defence Agreement to Scale Up Army, Navy Exercises, Establish Regular Dialogue," *CNA*, October 20, 2019.

Martin, Will, "The U.S. Could Lose Its Crown as the World's Most Powerful Economy as Soon as Next Year, and It's Unlikely to Ever Get It Back," *Business Insider*, January 10, 2019.

Ministry of Foreign Affairs of Japan, "Japan-Singapore Partnership Programme for the 21st Century (JSPP21) Planning Committee Meeting on the FY 2019 Annual Work Plan," press release, May 16, 2019. As of September 12, 2019: https://www.mofa.go.jp/press/release/press1e_000125.html

Nichols, Stafford, and Zacc Ritter, "U.S. Defense Promise Still Credible in Asia-Pacific," Gallup, July 17, 2018. As of June 23, 2020: https://news.gallup.com/poll/237209/defense-promise-credible-asia-pacific.aspx

Office of the United States Trade Representative, "Singapore," webpage, undated. As of October 23, 2019: https://ustr.gov/countries-regions/southeast-asia-pacific/Singapore

Pacific Air Forces, homepage, undated. As of June 25, 2020: https://www.pacaf.af.mil

Panda, Ankit, "Singapore: A Small Asian Heavyweight," Council on Foreign Relations, June 26, 2018. As of October 23, 2019: https://www.cfr.org/backgrounder/singapore-small-asian-heavyweight

Parameswaran, Prashanth, "Australia and Singapore: What's in a New Strategic Partnership?" *The Diplomat*, June 30, 2015. As of September 12, 2019: https://thediplomat.com/2015/06/australia-and-singapore-whats-in-a-new-strategic-partnership/

———, "Strengthening US-Singapore Strategic Partnership: Opportunities and Challenges," *RSIS Commentary*, August 8, 2016.

———, "US Air Force Exercise Kicks Off with Singapore's Participation," *The Diplomat*, August 17, 2017. As of September 12, 2019: https://thediplomat.com/2017/08/us-air-force-exercise-kicks-off-with-singapores-participation/

———, "Army Exercise Puts US-Singapore Defense Relations into Focus," *The Diplomat*, April 30, 2018. As of September 12, 2019: https://thediplomat.com/2018/04/army-exercise-puts-us-singapore-defense-relations-into-focus/

———, "Strategic Security Dialogue Highlights US-Singapore Defense Relations," *The Diplomat*, April 29, 2019a. As of September 12, 2019: https://thediplomat.com/2019/04/strategic-security-dialogue-highlights-us-singapore-defense-relations/

———, "What's in the New China-Singapore Deepening Military Ties Talk?" *The Diplomat*, May 30, 2019b. As of September 12, 2019: https://thediplomat.com/2019/05/whats-in-the-china-singapore-deepening-military-ties-talk/

———, "What's in the New US-Singapore Artificial Intelligence Defense Partnership?" *The Diplomat*, July 1, 2019c. As of September 12, 2019: https://thediplomat.com/2019/07/whats-in-the-new-us-singapore-artificial-intelligence-defense-partnership/

Pearlman, Jonathan, "Ministers Discuss Next Stages of SAF's Training Deal," *Straits Times*, March 30, 2019.

People's Republic of China, Ministry of Commerce, *2017 Statistical Bulletin of China's Outward Foreign Direct Investment*, October 2018. As of July 21, 2020: http://images.mofcom.gov.cn/hzs/201810/20181029160118046.pdf

Pew Research Center, Global Indicators Database, "Australia: Opinion of the United States," updated August 2017.

PricewaterhouseCoopers, *The Long View: How Will the Global Economic Order Change by 2050?* London, February 2017.

Qin, Amy, "Worries in Singapore Grow over China's Calls to Help 'Motherland,'" *New York Times*, August 5, 2018.

Reaffirming Singapore's Strategic Partnership with the United States, Encompassing Broad and Robust Economic, Military-to-Military, Law Enforcement, and Counterterrorism Cooperation, H.R. Res. 374, 114th Congress, July 12, 2016.

Republic of Singapore Air Force, "Overseas Training and Detachments," webpage, undated. As of October 23, 2019:
https://www.mindef.gov.sg/oms/rsaf/careers/about-us/training-experiences.html

Sim, Dewey, "Singapore Renews Military Bases Pact with US Amid Deepening Defence Ties with China," *South China Morning Post*, September 24, 2019a.

———, "Singapore Gets Fighter Jet Unit on Guam as US, Facing China Threat, Lauds Closer Ties with Allies," *South China Morning Post*, December 9, 2019b.

State Council of the People's Republic of China, *The Diversified Employment of China's Armed Forces*, Beijing, 2013.

———, *China's Foreign Aid*, Beijing, 2014.

———, *China's Military Strategy*, Beijing, 2015.

———, *China's Policies on Asia-Pacific Security Cooperation*, Beijing, 2017.

Stockholm International Peace Research Institute, "SIPRI Arms Transfers Database," webpage, undated a. As of July 21, 2020:
https://www.sipri.org/databases/armstransfers

———, "SIPRI Arms Transfers Database – Methodology," webpage, undated b. As of August 7, 2020:
https://www.sipri.org/databases/armstransfers/background

Stokes, Bruce, Dorothy Manevich, and Hanyu Chwe, "India and the World," Pew Research Center, November 15, 2017.

Su-Lyn, Boo, "Malaysians More Positive About China Now, Studies Show," *Malay Mail*, April 1, 2017.

Tang Siew Mun, Moe Thuzar, Hoang Thi Ha, Termsak Chalermpalanupap, Pham Thi Phuong Thao, and Anuthida Saelaow Qian, *The State of Southeast Asia: 2019 Survey Report*,

Singapore: ISEAS–Yusof Ishak Institute, 2019. As of September 12, 2019: https://www.iseas.edu.sg/medias/latest-news/item/8831-in-the-news-state-of-southeast-asia-2019-survey

Transparency International, "Corruption Perceptions Index: 2018," webpage, 2018. As of October 23, 2019: https://www.transparency.org/cpi2018

United Nations, "UN Comtrade Database," webpage, undated. As of July 21, 2020: https://comtrade.un.org

United Nations Conference on Trade and Development, *World Investment Report 2018: Investment and New Industrial Policies*, Geneva, Switzerland: United Nations Publications, 2018.

U.S. Army Pacific, homepage, undated. As of June 25, 2020: https://www.army.mil/usarpac

U.S. Bureau of Economic Analysis, "Direct Investment by Country and Industry," webpage, updated July 24, 2019. As of October 28, 2019: https://www.bea.gov/data/intl-trade-investment/direct-investment-country-and-industry

———, "Foreign Direct Investment in the U.S.: Balance of Payments and Direct Investment Position Data," webpage, updated June 19, 2020. As of June 25, 2020: https://www.bea.gov/international/di1fdibal

U.S. Department of Defense, *Assessment on U.S. Defense Implications of China's Expanding Global Access*, Washington, D.C.: Office of the Secretary of Defense, 6-6B48CD8, December 20, 2018.

———, *Annual Report to Congress: Military and Security Developments Involving the People's Republic of China 2019*, Washington, D.C.: Office of the Secretary of Defense, E-1F4B924, May 2, 2019.

U.S. Department of Defense and U.S. Department of State, *Fiscal Years 2017 and 2018 Joint Report to Congress*, Vol. 1, Washington, D.C., Foreign Military Training Report F-685A5A8, November 27, 2017a.

———, *Fiscal Years 2017 and 2018 Joint Report to Congress*, Vol. 2: *Country Training Activities*, Washington, D.C., Foreign Military Training Report F-685A5A8, November 27, 2017b.

———, *Fiscal Years 2018 and 2019 Joint Report to Congress*, Vol. 1, Washington, D.C., Foreign Military Training Report 2-C52504A, March 13, 2019a.

———, *Fiscal Years 2018 and 2019 Joint Report to Congress*, Vol. 2: *Country Training Activities*, Washington, D.C., Foreign Military Training Report 2-C52504A, March 13, 2019b.

U.S. Department of State, homepage, undated a. As of June 24, 2020:
https://www.state.gov

———, "Press Releases," webpage, undated b. As of June 24, 2020:
https://www.state.gov/press-releases/

———, "Websites of U.S. Embassies, Consulates, and Diplomatic Missions," webpage, undated c. As of June 24, 2020:
https://www.usembassy.gov

White House, "Barack Obama," webpage, undated a. As of June 24, 2020:
https://www.whitehouse.gov/about-the-white-house/presidents/barack-obama/

———, "Briefings & Statements," webpage, undated b. As of June 24, 2020:
https://www.whitehouse.gov/briefings-statements/

———, "George W. Bush," webpage, undated c. As of June 24, 2020:
https://www.whitehouse.gov/about-the-white-house/presidents/george-w-bush/

"The World's Economic Powerhouses Are Going to Look Very Different in Another Decade," *News.com.au,* January 20, 2019.

Yong, Charissa, "Should Small States Act Like Small States?" *Straits Times*, July 9, 2017. As of July 21, 2020:
https://www.straitstimes.com/singapore/should-small-states-act-like-small-states